GALATIANS
The Beating Heart of the Gospel

Roy W. Hefti

A Devotional Commentary

NORTHWESTERN PUBLISHING HOUSE
Milwaukee, Wisconsin

Cover: Image used under license from iStock.com
Design: Amy Malo

Scripture quotations are from the Holy Bible, Evangelical Heritage Version®
(EHV®) ©2019 Wartburg Project, Inc. All rights reserved. Used by permission.

All hymns, unless otherwise indicated, are taken from *Christian Worship:
Hymnal* © 2021 by Northwestern Publishing House.

"Lines From Luther" chapters 1-9 are from *Luther's Works*, American Edition,
Vol. 26 © 1963, 1991 Concordia Publishing House. Used with permission.

"Lines From Luther" chapters 10-13 are from *Luther's Works*, American Edition,
Vol. 27 © 1964, 1992 Concordia Publishing House. Used with permission.

Northwestern Publishing House
N16W23379 Stone Ridge Dr., Waukesha WI 53188-1108
www.nph.net
© 2024 by Northwestern Publishing House
Published 2024
Printed in the United States of America
ISBN 978-0-8100-3243-9
ISBN 978-0-8100-3244-6 (e-book)

24 25 26 27 28 29 30 31 32 33   10 9 8 7 6 5 4 3 2 1

To Ali, my beloved

Introduction

Like Paul's letter to the Romans, his letter to the Galatians deals with the chief article of the Christian faith—justification by faith in Christ alone. In this letter we see uncovered the beating heart of the gospel.

But the tone of these six chapters is far different than that of Romans. Here the smoke of battle and the clatter of weaponry rise from the page. Unlike Paul's calmer and more studied approach in his letter to the Romans, we can sense the apostle's burning passion to cut to the chase.

That is because a crisis arose among the Galatian churches soon after Paul's second missionary tour among them.

Some professing believers, people who came to be called the Judaizers, infiltrated the ranks, hearts, and minds of the Galatian believers. They possibly came from the Jerusalem church and certainly claimed to be followers of Jesus, but they insisted that a person must also keep the ceremonial laws of the Sinai or Mosaic covenant to be saved. In short, they would tell gentile (non-Jewish) people that they must first become Jewish before they could become Christian. They told these new converts to Christ, "Unless you are circumcised according to the law handed down by Moses, you cannot be saved" (Acts 15:1).

Like many churches throughout history and in our own day, the Judaizers did not deny that people should believe Jesus died for their sins and rose again. But they did maintain that faith in

Christ was not enough. They preached that obedience to the law, specifically to the ceremonial laws of Moses, was part of one's salvation. Instead of proclaiming salvation by faith in Christ alone, they said that salvation came by faith *and* works.

In this letter Paul drives a wooden stake through the heart of this false teaching. The book of Galatians has been called the Magna Carta of Christian liberty. It has been labeled the hammer, sword, and battle cry of the Lutheran Reformation. Martin Luther's best known Bible commentary, even more famous than his many volumes on Genesis, is his commentary on Galatians. In one of his informal "table talks," he once said, "The epistle to the Galatians is my epistle. To it I am, as it were, in wedlock. It is my Katherine" (a reference to Luther's dear wife, Katie).

The pages that follow grew gradually out of sermons I preached in 2012 at St. Paul's Evangelical Lutheran Church in Bangor, Wisconsin, where I was honored to serve as pastor (1984–2020). This commentary aims to be devotional, practical, and plain to the ordinary reader while being mindful of the Greek text behind the English translation (Evangelical Heritage Version). At the close of each section, selected quotations from Luther's commentary on Galatians are provided.

Let us, like Luther, bind these six chapters to our hearts, fight once more the good fight of faith, and lay hold of the eternal life in Christ.

Pastor Roy W. Hefti

GALATIANS
The Beating Heart of the Gospel

Contents

GALATIANS

1:1-10
No Other Gospel

The God-breathed books of the New Testament are epistles, letters. They are not dry and dusty doctrinal essays. Letters are not written in a vacuum. There's always a backstory to them. Think of a combat soldier's letter to his wife, a parent's letter to a confused child at college, or a pastor's letter to a troubled soul who has moved far from home.

There is a backstory too behind Paul's letter to the Christians in southern Galatia. On Paul's first missionary journey, he establishes several congregations in ancient Asia Minor (modern-day Turkey). Some of the names may ring a bell from the New Testament book of Acts—places such as Antioch, Iconium, Lystra, and Derbe. These churches in southern Galatia have both Jewish and gentile converts to Christ. On the way home from his first journey, Paul retraces his steps, reinforces the gospel message in these infant congregations, and sees to it that church leaders (elders, pastors, and teachers) are put in place. Paul is no fly-by-night, showbiz-for-Jesus preacher. He plants the pure gospel of Jesus Christ. He waters and cultivates the seed of the

Word with thorough instruction in the teachings of the Bible. He establishes congregations that will bear fruit long after he has moved on. On his second missionary journey, he passes through Galatia again, strengthening and encouraging these new believers. Then he moves on to Macedonia and Greece.

What happens after Paul's departure from the Galatians is the story behind this fiery and feisty epistle. Paul mentions how quickly it happened. He has just settled into his ministry in the Greek city of Corinth when he gets word that troublemakers have infiltrated the Galatian churches. These troublemakers are known to church history as the Judaizers. These are Jews who declare themselves converted to Christianity but maintain that faith in Christ is not enough.

The controversy is not a new one. Acts chapter 15 describes a meeting in Jerusalem where the apostles deal with it. The Judaizers state their position bluntly, "Unless you are circumcised according to the law handed down by Moses, you cannot be saved" (Acts 15:1). For the Judaizers, circumcision represents the entire Old Testament ceremonial code of Moses. These ceremonies and regulations, however, were all fulfilled in Christ. They were fading shadows of things to come (Colossians 2:16,17). Even the Old Testament believers knew they were not saved by keeping such laws. They trusted in the coming Christ for their salvation. Yet the Judaizers assert that the Gentiles can become Christian only by first becoming Jewish, by being circumcised and keeping the laws of Moses. Speaking for the apostles, Peter states the correct position just as bluntly, "We believe that we are saved in the same way they are—through the grace of our Lord Jesus" (Acts 15:11).

You would think that the controversy is now settled. Salvation is by grace alone through faith in Christ alone, apart from works of the law. But error, once voted down, forever brings the matter up for another vote. Paul cuts to the chase in these opening lines of his letter to the Galatians. He declares that there is no other gospel than the one he has already proclaimed—no matter how appealing false gospels may appear.

Paul's very greeting to the Galatians reminds them that there is no other gospel than the one he has already proclaimed.

> ¹:¹**Paul, an apostle—not from men, nor through a man, but through Jesus Christ and God the Father, who raised him from the dead—²and all of the brothers who are with me,**
>
> **To the churches of Galatia:**
>
> ³**Grace to you and peace from God our Father and the Lord Jesus Christ. ⁴He gave himself for our sins to rescue us from this present evil age, according to the will of our God and Father—⁵to whom be the glory forever and ever. Amen.**

Paul usually begins his letters with some words of encouragement and a word of thanks to God for the faith and the fruits of faith worked in the believers' hearts through the gospel. Even in the case of his problem-child congregation at Corinth, he commends before he corrects. He encourages before he criticizes.

Not this time. The present crisis trumps everything. Paul gets to the point. He underlines his divine call as an apostle, as one sent directly by Christ and who speaks the very Word of Christ. That's because the Judaizers have undermined his message, as we shall see, by questioning his authority. "Who is this Paul," they argue, "this Johnny-come-lately to the party? Paul is not one of the twelve original disciples who walked with Christ during his earthly ministry. Paul may have given you a good start, but he left a lot of blanks that we will now fill in for you." Paul counters this. He calls himself a genuine apostle of Christ. "Not from men," he says, that is, not from human origin. Here Paul has in mind self-appointed preachers who have no divine call or authority at all, neither directly from God nor indirectly through the church. Such self-appointed preachers usually claim some direct pipeline to God that the Holy Spirit has whispered in their ears. Luther called such false teachers in his day fanatics or "enthusiasts" and labeled their activity *Schwaermerei*, a German word which refers to the busy buzzing of bees—all noise, no substance—placing themselves above the Bible and sacraments as sources of spiritual truth. Today we are flooded with false teachers who name their so-called ministries after themselves, turn up their noses at the meat and potatoes of Christ's Word, and claim a fuller revelation.

"On the contrary," says Paul, "I am sent not *from* men," not by some human notion, "nor *through* a man," referring to the indirect call that people may have through the church as we do today, a legitimate call from God through a group of believers. "Rather," says Paul, "I am an *apostle* . . . through Jesus Christ and God the Father, who raised him from the dead." Like Moses, Isaiah, and the twelve apostles, Paul was called directly by Christ himself, who appeared to him on the Damascus road in blinding glory (Acts chapter 9), by the risen Christ who directly taught him.

"Grace to you and peace," Paul says. That's the height and depth of it. Grace is God's undeserved love, a free gift, not just something for nothing but the opposite of what sinful people have got coming. Peace is the breaking down of the wall between God and us and the restoring of the way things are supposed to be between God and us. In short, grace forgives sin, and peace stills the conscience. Peace with God is impossible unless sin has been forgiven.

Who alone has grace and peace in his hands? Who else but God? "Grace to you and peace from God our Father," says Paul, "*and* the Lord Jesus Christ." Grace and peace come equally from the Father and the Lord Jesus Christ because Christ is God himself. Who would want a Savior who is less than God himself?

What did this Savior do for us? He "gave himself for our sins." These are loaded words. If we could earn our way into the arms of the Father by our own goodness, then why would Christ give himself for our sins? Nor should we miss the sermon Paul preaches with the single pronoun *our*. Christ "gave himself for *our* sins." We may believe easily enough that Jesus died for the sins of Peter, Paul, or some other hero of faith, but it is very hard some days, when conscience and Satan come to call, to believe that Christ died for *our* sins.

Lay hold of this. Cultivate this in your heart by staying close to the gospel, the good news. Christ did not die for minor sins (for no sin is minor), fake sins (which we may confess with pretend humility), or one or two sins (which for whatever reason do not seem to bother us). Christ died for big sins, for real sins, for all sins, for our sins, for your sins, for the sins we recall and the sins we have forgotten, for the sins out there that people see and the sins here, in our hearts, that we and God alone know.

This is the real gospel, and there is no other gospel than the good news that Christ "gave himself for our sins to rescue us from this present evil age" in which we find ourselves every day. All this Christ did for us and for all. He has brought us to believe this, not because we willed or decided it but by the will of our God and Father who loved us before we knew him. To him be the glory forever and ever for this gospel, the greatest of good news.

For there is no other gospel, no matter how appealing fake gospels may appear.

⁶I am amazed that you are so quickly deserting the one who called you in the grace of Christ, for a different gospel, ⁷which is really not another gospel at all. There are, however, some who are trying to disturb you by perverting the gospel of Christ. ⁸But even if we or an angel from heaven would preach any gospel

other than the one we preached to you—a curse on
him! ⁹As we have said before, so I now say again: If
anyone preaches to you any gospel other than the one
you received—a curse on him! ¹⁰Am I now seeking the
favor of people or of God? Or am I striving to please
people? If I were still trying to gain the approval of
people, I would not be a servant of Christ.

Did you notice that Paul speaks in one tone to his parishioners and in another tone to the false teachers? To the Galatians
themselves he talks like a loving parent who is surprised and
disappointed at a child's behavior: "I am amazed that you are so
quickly deserting the one who called you." There is a parental
sort of pain in Paul's rebuke coupled with a confidence that it is
not too late to call the Galatian Christians back. They are in the
process of deserting, forsaking, and abandoning the Christ who
called them, but they have not totally gone over the edge.

But against the false teachers who have infected the flock,
Paul comes out with guns blazing. It is like a high noon shoot-out
at the O. K. Corral. In Luther's famous commentary on Galatians, he notes this contrast between the way Paul speaks to the
Galatians and the way he speaks to the Judaizers. Luther says
that when a child has been bitten by a dog, the parents chase the
dog but console the child.

Paul is astonished that the Galatians have deserted the
gospel so quickly. As mere infants in the faith, they are tossed
back and forth by every wind of doctrine (Ephesians 4:14).
A faith lightly held is a faith lightly dropped. Luther remarks that
a preacher can spend ten years setting a confused congregation
in order, and the whole thing can be ruined overnight by some
slick false prophet.

The Galatians have allowed themselves to get drunk on a
different gospel, which is no gospel at all. (The Greek word here

for "different" is part of the English word *heterodoxy*, a teaching that is different from what the Word of God teaches.) The false teachers who trouble them are distorting the gospel, polluting it with work-righteousness, an attempt to achieve righteousness through human effort. Authentic (confessional) Lutheran pastors see this frequently—members who tire of their plain-Jane Lutheranism and are seduced by more glamorous self-help gospels in which Jesus is the footnote and the good news is about us and what we are doing rather than what Christ has done.

Calling such a message "the gospel" does not make it the gospel. As a young lawyer, Abraham Lincoln once asked a man on the witness stand, "If you call a dog's tail a leg, how many legs does the dog have?" The man answered, "Well, if you call a dog's tail a leg, then I suppose he's got five legs." Lincoln replied, "Wrong! He's still got four legs, because calling a tail a leg doesn't make it one." Calling a false gospel the gospel doesn't make it the gospel.

Paul hurls a divine curse on the Judaizers who have dimmed the glory of Christ and have poisoned the faith of the Galatians. He says, "Even if we or an angel from heaven would preach any gospel other than the one we preached to you—a curse on him!" He then repeats it, "If anyone preaches to you any gospel other than the one you received—a curse on him!" The word for "curse" is literally *anathema*, something under a curse, devoted to destruction, like the city of Jericho in Joshua's day (Joshua 6:26; 1 Kings 16:34). Paul here echoes the severe curses of God's holy law pronounced by the psalmists and prophets of the Old Testament and by Christ himself (Matthew 23:13-39; Luke 11:37-52). Those who lead others to hell with a false gospel pave the path to hell for themselves.

Tough words, Paul admits, but he is not seeking the approval of people. Paul will not tailor God's truth to be popular. One cannot be a people pleaser and a servant of Christ at the same time. In the chapters to come in this epistle, we shall find a real gospel for real sinners. For all of us who are troubled by memories of our past sins, who are craving strength for our present weaknesses, or who are fearful of future failures, there is no other gospel. Thank God.

Lines From Luther

Grace and peace—these two words embrace the whole of Christianity. Grace forgives sin, and peace stills the conscience. . . . Peace is impossible unless sin has first been forgiven. (*Luther's Works*, Vol. 26, p. 26)

Pay careful attention to Paul's every word, and note particularly this pronoun "our." For we find very often in the Scriptures that their significance consists in the proper application of pronouns, which also convey vigor and force. It is easy for you to say and believe that Christ, the Son of God, was given for the sins of Peter, Paul, and other saints, who seem to us to have been worthy of this grace. But it is very hard for you, who regard yourself as unworthy of this grace, to say and believe from your heart that Christ was given for *your* many great sins. . . . Therefore you must not think of them as minor or suppose that your own works can remove them. Nor must you despair on account of their gravity if you feel them oppressing you either in life or in death. But you must learn from Paul here to believe that Christ was given, not for sham or counterfeit sins, nor yet for small sins, but for great and huge sins; not for one or two sins but for all sins; not for sins that have been overcome—for neither man nor angel is able to overcome even the tiniest sin—but for invincible sins. (*Luther's Works*, Vol. 26, pp. 33-35)

But anyone who does not get rid of the memory of his sin but holds on to it and tortures himself with his own thoughts, supposing either that he can help himself by his own strength or that he can wait until his conscience has been pacified, falls into Satan's trap. . . . Learn this definition carefully. Especially practice this pronoun "our" in such a way that this syllable, once believed, may swallow up and absorb all your sins, that is, that you may be certain that Christ has taken away not only the sins of some men but your sins and those of the whole world. The offering was for the sins of the whole world, even though the whole world does not believe. (*Luther's Works*, Vol. 26, pp. 37,38)

A man may labor for a decade before he puts some small church into proper order. And once it is in order, along comes some fanatic who cannot do anything but slander and abuse the sincere preachers of the Word— and in one moment he overthrows everything! Who would not be agitated by such outrageous actions? (*Luther's Works*, Vol. 26, p. 45)

But the holier the heretics seem to be in external appearance, the more damage they cause. (*Luther's Works*, Vol. 26, p. 52)

GALATIANS

1:11-24
The Revealed Gospel

I n the mid-1700s, two Englishmen named Gilbert West and George Lyttelton tried something as trendy then in the so-called age of rationalism as it is today in the so-called age of postmodernism. They set out to discredit Christianity.

They painted bull's-eyes on two major events recorded in the New Testament: the bodily resurrection of Jesus Christ and the miraculous conversion of Paul by the risen Christ on the road to Damascus. If they could disprove these two events, then the entire New Testament, and Christianity with it, would collapse.

West was to play myth buster on the resurrection of Christ. Lyttelton was to debunk the conversion of Paul. The two intelligent skeptics went their separate ways and gave it their best shot. Eventually they got together to compare notes. First one, then the other, sheepishly confessed to have changed views entirely. Each was compelled to defend the biblical record rather than attack it. West's book was entitled *Observations on the History and Evidences of the Resurrection of Jesus Christ*. Lyttelton wrote a defense of the Christian faith entitled *Observations on the Conversion and Apostleship of St. Paul.*

Many assaults have been made on Paul's conversion over the years, but like the attacks on Christ's resurrection, these arrogant tactics have, to lift a line from the poet Lord Byron, "melted like snow in the glance of the Lord" ("The Destruction of Sennacherib"). Each generation's mocking magazine articles or TV documentaries of doubt are soon forgotten on the scrap heap of history. The Bible remains.

But you can see—can't you?—why the anti-Christian snipers take aim at Paul's conversion? Discredit the risen Christ's glorious appearance to Paul, and you discredit Paul himself as an inspired apostle. Do that and you discredit the 13 books of the New Testament that Paul wrote.

The anti-Christian snipers in Paul's own day were called the Judaizers. These were Jews who professed Christianity but insisted that faith in Christ was not enough. They asserted the necessity of observing Old Testament ceremonial laws that Christ had already fulfilled. Chief among their requirements for salvation was the religious rite of circumcision.

This so-called gospel with small print at the bottom of the page is no gospel at all, says Paul. A conditional good news is a counterfeit good news. The genuine gospel of God's free grace does not come with the shipping and handling charges of human effort.

In the opening lines of this letter to the Galatians, Paul has fired the opening salvo at these Judaizers, who are peddling this polluted gospel to the congregations he founded in southern Galatia. He thunders, "Even if we or an angel from heaven would preach any gospel other than the one we preached to you—a curse on him!" (Galatians 1:8).

Nonetheless, in the verses that follow Paul takes a more tender tone with his beloved Galatians, who have been duped and bewitched by these pious frauds. He offers an antidote to the infiltrators who have suggested to the Galatians that he is a second-rate, Johnny-come-lately to the glorious company of Christ's original apostles. Paul points out that the gospel he preaches is the gospel directly revealed to him by the risen Savior—revealed to the least likely candidate by grace alone and to the glory of God alone.

Paul asserts that the gospel was directly revealed to him by Christ himself.

> [11]**I want you to know, brothers, that the gospel I preached is not of human origin.** [12]**For I did not receive it from man, nor was I taught it, but I received it through a revelation from Jesus Christ.**

If you have read the book of Acts, then you know the story behind Paul's claim about the gospel he preaches. The apostle had gone by the name Saul. The Bible says, "Saul was trying to destroy the church by going into one house after another, dragging off both men and women, and putting them in prison" (Acts 8:3).

But Saul is not content to scatter the disciples in Jerusalem. He requisitions official letters, arrest warrants, and an escort of temple guards to head 135 miles north to Damascus. Word has reached him of Jews in the synagogue there who had converted to Christianity.

Just outside Damascus, Saul's crusade against the Christians is interrupted. He is caught up in a brilliant light by a blinding appearance of the risen Lord Jesus Christ himself, who asks him, "Saul, Saul, why are you persecuting me?"

"Who are you, Lord?" Saul asks. Then comes the answer: "I am Jesus, whom you are persecuting. But get up and go into the city, and you will be told what you need to do" (Acts 9:4-6).

This is the story behind Paul's assertion about the gospel revealed to him. "It is not of human origin," he tells the Galatians.

It is not some self-help philosophy invented by humans. "In fact," says Paul, "I did not, as most believers do, receive it from man. I was not taught it. Nobody sat me down for a course of instruction. No, I received it through a direct revelation from Jesus Christ."

"If you consider what I once was," says Paul, "then you would agree that it would take more than a few thoughts borrowed from someone else to make me what I am today." The gospel was revealed to the least likely candidate.

[13]Certainly you have heard of my former way of life in Judaism, how I used to persecute the church of God to an extraordinary degree and tried to destroy it. [14]I was advancing in Judaism beyond many of my contemporaries among my own people, because I was extremely zealous for the traditions of my fathers.

Paul points the Galatians to what he used to be to demonstrate what it would take to make him what he is.

Paul, or Saul, was a native of Tarsus in Asia Minor, a city of perhaps half a million, a university town. Tarsus was declared a free city by the Romans. This made Saul a Roman citizen while also being a devout Jew. As a young man, he studied at the feet of the famous Jewish teacher Gamaliel. Like Gamaliel, he became a Pharisee, a member of that self-righteous sect always in the face of Jesus in the gospel accounts.

Saul was not a drunkard or a swindler. He knew his Old Testament Scriptures like the back of his hand. But he was a self-righteous man, "a Pharisee, a son of Pharisees" as he called himself (Acts 23:6). He sought salvation by works of obedience rather than by God's free grace, God's undeserved love. Saul was bent on the destruction of the people who proclaimed Jesus of Nazareth as the promised Savior and Messiah. He believed with all his heart that Jesus was an impostor. He believed that Jesus was dead and rotting in his grave. That was the fate he wanted for the followers of Jesus too.

As Saul nears Damascus, he is having no second thoughts about persecuting Christians. He is in no way disposed to make a decision for Christ, as though a person could do this. If something is to change in this man, it will have to be all God's doing—a direct revelation—for this man is the least likely convert and the least likely candidate for the apostolic ministry.

So as with all of us, the gospel is revealed by grace alone.

[15]However, God, who set me apart from my mother's womb and called me by his grace, was pleased [16]to reveal his Son in me, so that I would preach him among the Gentiles. At that time, I did not immediately consult with flesh and blood, [17]and I did not go up to Jerusalem to those who were apostles before me. Instead I went away into Arabia, and then I returned again to Damascus.

Grace was the theme of the apostle Paul. Listen to the way Paul talks: "God, who set me apart from my mother's womb and called me by his grace, was pleased to reveal his Son in me, so that I would preach him among the Gentiles." "Before I could have a single thought about the whole thing," says Paul, "God set me apart, drew a circle around me, set his love on me, raised my cold, dead heart to life by the CPR of this revealed gospel, and called me to be an apostle—one sent by Christ to speak the words of Christ."

"From my mother's womb." While this is true in a special way of Paul's apostleship, or of Jeremiah's prophetic office (Jeremiah 1:4,5), our own call to faith by this revealed gospel is just as much by grace. Maybe you come before God with a long-term worry, with a burden of helplessness. God's grace assures you that there is some sort of order in your life. Yes, there are detours on the journey; potholes in the path you never planned on; disappointments, diseases, and failures that throw a monkey wrench into your dreams. You may think that things are always just happening to you, as though God is not really clued in, does not truly understand your situation. But things are not just happening. He who drew a circle around you with his love before you were born, who affirmed that love in blood on a cross, who made the good news of his Easter victory yours through faith—he is not writing a meaningless tragedy but an adventure in which the last, happy chapter is already written.

It is this revealed gospel that Paul now preaches to the glory of God.

> [18]Next, after three years, I went up to Jerusalem to meet Cephas and stayed with him fifteen days. [19]But I saw none of the other apostles, except James, the Lord's brother. [20](Now about the things I am writing to you—look, I assure you in the presence of God that I am not lying.) [21]Then I went to the regions of Syria and Cilicia. [22]I was still personally unknown to the churches of Judea that are in Christ. [23]They heard only: "The one who was once persecuting us is now preaching the faith that he once tried to destroy." [24]And they were praising God for what happened to me.

Paul leaves Damascus after his dramatic conversion and call. He goes to an area southeast of Damascus known as Stony Arabia. Did he preach the gospel there to the sparse children of the desert? Did he receive additional revelations and instruction from Jesus himself? Was it here that Paul received the vision he speaks of years later in 2 Corinthians 12:2-4, when he was "carried up to the third heaven" and heard things he couldn't even put into human words? We are not told.

Eventually Paul returns to Damascus, preaches the gospel there, and then flees for his life. Three years after his conversion, he goes up to Jerusalem to meet Cephas—the Aramaic name for the apostle Peter. Paul stays there only 15 days. He sees none of the other apostles, except James, the Lord's brother, who heads up the church in Jerusalem. Then Paul is off to Syria and Cilicia—his old boyhood haunts.

For years, most Christians in Judea didn't even know Paul by face. He neither needed nor requested any sort of certification or accreditation from the other apostles. The gospel was revealed directly to Paul. He was a bona fide apostle in his own right. The other apostles recognized this. They glorified God because of it. Later, they fully supported his missionary journeys to the Gentiles—yes, to the Galatians too.

The Galatian Christians need to know that they already have the revealed gospel. They need no other gospel, no new and improved gospel. We today need no modernized, more entertaining, self-help gospel either. We need to believe the genuine gospel we already have. The gospel revealed to Paul lies open in our hands, written as revealed by the breath of God (2 Timothy 3:16; 2 Peter 1:21). And as those two Englishmen discovered long ago, it has not lost its ancient touch or saving power. This is the Book of books about which one poet wrote:

Last eve I passed beside the blacksmith's door,
And heard the anvil ring the vesper chime.
And looking in, I saw upon the floor,
Old hammers, worn with beating years of time.

"How many anvils have you had," said I,
"To wear and batter all these hammers so?"
"Just one," said he, and then with twinkling eye,
"The anvil wears the hammers out, you know."
And so, thought I, the anvil of God's Word—
For ages skeptic blows have beat upon.
But though the noise of falling blows was heard,
The anvil is unharmed, the hammers gone.

—attrib. John Clifford

Lines From Luther

When Paul denies that he received his Gospel from man, he clearly indicates by this that Christ is not a mere man but is true God and man at the same time. (*Luther's Works*, Vol. 26, p. 62)

I recall that when my movement first began, Dr. Staupitz [Johann von Staupitz, Luther's superior and mentor in the monastery], a very worthy man and the vicar of the Augustinian Order, said to me: "It pleases me very much that this doctrine of ours gives glory and everything else solely to God and nothing at all to men; for it is as clear as day that it is impossible to ascribe too much glory, goodness, etc. to God." (*Luther's Works*, Vol. 26, p. 66)

For no one likes to say that the church is in error; and yet, if the church teaches anything in addition or contrary to the Word of God, one must say that it is in error. (*Luther's Works*, Vol. 26, pp. 66,67)

2:1-10
The Right Hand of Fellowship

The fellowship of believers was threatened at the very start of the New Testament age. Sadly, the fellowship of the visible church has been destroyed many times in many places.

But there is a perfect fellowship of kindred hearts that can never be destroyed. We confess it regularly in the Apostle's Creed, "I believe in . . . the holy Christian Church, the communion [Greek: *koinonia*—"fellowship"] of saints." The holy Christian Church or communion of saints is really the one true church. It is made up of all believers in Christ—and only of believers in Christ. This is worth repeating: All those who believe in Jesus Christ alone as their Savior from sin are members of this one holy Christian Church, the communion or fellowship of saints— that is, believers—regardless of the race, nation, or church body to which they belong. It is an unscriptural and indefensible notion that only those who belong to some particular church body are going to heaven.

We call the one holy Christian Church by another name, the invisible church, because its membership is known only to God.

Only God knows who truly believes in Jesus as the only Savior. We rejoice to know that there are believers all over the world in many different Christian churches and that all Christians will enjoy perfect fellowship in heaven.

But the invisible church is a gathering of hearts that only God can see. You and I are not God, so you and I can only deal with the visible church. If you invite people to church next Sunday and they say, "Sure, where is it?" it won't be much help to say, "Well, it's invisible."

So when we want to know where to find believers in Christ, we look for what the church fathers called the marks of the church. If you live in deer hunting country, think of it as the tracks of the church, namely, the signs or tracks that show the church is present. What are the marks or tracks of the church? The gospel purely preached and the sacraments rightly administered. There God's Word will not return empty. We expect to find fellow believers, even though hypocrites may be mingled in that visible gathering.

So here we are, living out our lives in the visible church, painfully aware that there have been tragic divisions in congregations from the very beginning and church bodies that were once orthodox or right-teaching no longer are. The so-called ecumenical movement, with its emphasis on external church unity and cooperation, ended up promoting unionism, an outward union without true unity in the teachings of the Bible. Its answer is to agree to disagree; to pretend that doctrinal differences are no big deal; to gather everyone under one big umbrella to share worship, preaching, and prayer activities without first agreeing on what the Bible teaches—all in the name of love and tolerance.

The trouble is, such an approach is not as loving as it sounds. It is lacking in love for God and his Word, the souls of others, and our own souls. Such compromise is a dangerous deception, a bridge to a false fellowship, a union without unity, a poisoned food for hungry souls.

Paul understands this as well as anyone. Doctrinal error has been injected into the congregations he founded in Galatia. The ability to acknowledge and enjoy true fellowship is endangered. In these verses, Paul takes the Galatians back to the discussion and decision of a council in Jerusalem to remind them of how the right hand of fellowship had been threatened, defended, and strengthened.

Recall the threat: Paul hears that troublemakers, the Judaizers, have infiltrated the Galatian churches. They maintain that mere faith in Christ is not enough. This threat to acknowledging and enjoying fellowship is nothing new. Paul reminds his beloved Galatian Christians of previous conversations and a meeting at Jerusalem regarding the same issue.

²:¹Then, after fourteen years, I went up again to Jerusalem with Barnabas, also taking Titus with me.

Paul relates that he went to Jerusalem, along with his missionary companion Barnabas and a gentile minister named Titus. Private conversations took place there between Paul and the leaders of the predominantly Jewish congregation in Jerusalem, presumably James, Peter, and John. Paul stresses that he went to Jerusalem in response to a direct revelation or command of God. Sometime after these conversations, Paul also participated in the meeting mentioned in Acts chapter 15. His words to the Galatians probably refer to the private discussions that preceded the formal meeting, but all his efforts in Jerusalem were to defend and clarify the doctrine and fellowship that were being threatened in Galatia.

²I went up in keeping with a revelation, and I laid before them the gospel that I preach among the Gentiles. But I did this privately before those who were considered important, in order to make sure that I was not running—or had not run—in vain. ³But Titus, who was with me, was not compelled to be circumcised, even though he is Greek. ⁴This was an issue because of the false brothers, who slipped in under false pretenses to spy on the freedom we have in Christ Jesus. Their goal was to make us slaves. ⁵We refused to give in to them even for a moment, so that the truth of the gospel would continue with you.

In essence, this is how Paul addresses the Galatians: "I didn't go up to Jerusalem because I was summoned by the other apostles or even because I thought I should go. I went to Jerusalem by the revelation and at the command of Christ himself. I went there to lay on the table the gospel I had been preaching for years to the gentile world.

"I met first with those who seemed to be influential, that is, the apostles and James, the brother of the Lord, who was the head of the Jerusalem church. I did this privately at first so there would be no misunderstanding as to why I was there, so that my gospel ministry, my running the race, would not be for nothing.

"And as it turned out, my meeting with the apostles and other leaders in Jerusalem demolished the Judaizers' lie that I have been preaching a different gospel than the other apostles. Clearly, we were all united in the law-free gospel of God's grace in Christ.

"As a matter of fact, not even Pastor Titus, a Greek—a non-Jew!—who was with me, was forced to be circumcised. Obviously, my fellow apostles saw no need of it. Clearly this different gospel with which you Galatians have been infected did not come from the apostles, did it?

"So, my dear Galatian brothers and sisters, where did you get this nonsense? You got it from those false teachers, didn't you? They came in secretly as stealth preachers, slipping in under the radar, speaking of Christ, sounding for all the world like Christian teachers. Yes, they spoke to you of Christ and the Scriptures. That's how false prophets work. They do not start by denying the existence of God or the value of the Bible. The wolves do not come in wolves' clothing but in sheep's clothing. Of course you didn't see big signs hung around their necks saying, 'Look out for us. We are false prophets!' Still, after I left, these Judaizers showed up to spy out your liberty in Christ, to enslave you to a religion of works rather than faith in the doing and dying of Christ.

"When the Judaizers tried to speak up in Jerusalem, we didn't give in to them for a moment. The other apostles and I knew what was at stake: the gospel itself. This business about circumcision and keeping the Law of Moses in order to be saved is a litmus test. If we caved in on this issue, if we failed to defend the foundation of fellowship in holding to the pure gospel, we would have lost the whole truth of Christ." This is how Paul speaks to his beloved Galatians.

In fact, when Paul met with the other apostles in Jerusalem, this gift of fellowship, so threatened by the Judaizers, was not only defended but strengthened.

⁶But as for those who were considered to be important (what sort of people they once were makes no difference to me; God shows no partiality), indeed, those who were considered to be important added nothing to my gospel. ⁷On the contrary, they saw that I had been entrusted with the gospel for the uncircumcised, just as Peter was entrusted with the gospel for the circumcised. ⁸For God, who worked effectively in

> **Peter to serve as an apostle to the circumcised, also worked effectively in me to serve as an apostle to the Gentiles. ⁹And because James, Cephas, and John, who were considered to be pillars, perceived the grace that was given to me, they gave Barnabas and me the right hand of fellowship. They agreed that we were to go to the Gentiles and they to the circumcised. ¹⁰The only thing they asked was that we remember the poor, the very thing that I was also eager to do.**

Civil governments have learned from both history and bitter experience that peace comes through strength, not through compromise and weakness. British Prime Minister Neville Chamberlain was willing to let Adolf Hitler have another piece of real estate in exchange for what he called "peace in our time." A colleague named Winston Churchill saw the matter more clearly and said, "Each one hopes that if he feeds the crocodile enough, the crocodile will eat him last."

So Paul reminds the Galatians that real unity among the apostles was based on the Word of God, not self-styled compromise. He says, "It was a wonderful thing that happened there in Jerusalem. The other apostles saw how God entrusted me with a ministry primarily to the uncircumcised, that is, to the Gentiles, just as Christ had entrusted Peter with a ministry primarily to the circumcised, that is, to the Jews. We all saw that we had a division of labor, not a division of doctrine."

"In fact," says Paul, "when James, Peter, and John saw the grace God had given me to preach to you Galatians and other Gentiles, they reached out to Barnabas and me with the right hand of fellowship, agreeing to this division of labor. They asked only that we remember the poor, a thing I am always eager to do in a world where so many of the Lord's people are not rich and famous but often poor and persecuted."

This is Paul's tactful touch on the hearts of the Galatian Christians who have been fooled by the slippery talk and flattery of the Judaizers. We see here how holding to the truth of God's Word at all costs is what really strengthens the right hand of fellowship among us—what really sets us free as Jesus himself said. We also observe that it is error that divides and truth that unites.

The prophet Isaiah pictures the church as a tent. He encourages God's people, "Make your tent ropes longer. Make your tent stakes stronger" (Isaiah 54:2). Before we can lengthen the cords to make a bigger tent, we must strengthen the stakes, making sure the tent is securely anchored in the firm foundation of the Scriptures. Then with great joy we will also lengthen the cords of the tent to spread the shade of Christ's gospel over others. May God deliver us from every snare, large or small, that would rob us of this fellowship with him and with one another!

Lines From Luther

But faith in its proper function has no other object than Jesus Christ, the Son of God, who was put to death for the sins of the world. It does not look at its love and say: "What have I done? Where have I sinned? What have I deserved?" But it says: "What has Christ done? What has He deserved?" (*Luther's Works*, Vol. 26, p. 88)

For if faith is to be sure and firm, it must take hold of nothing but Christ alone; and in the agony and terror of conscience it has nothing else to lean on than this pearl of great value (Matt. 13:45-46). Therefore whoever takes hold of Christ by faith, no matter how terrified by the Law and oppressed by the burden of his sins he may be, has the right to boast that he is righteous. How has he this right? By that jewel, Christ, whom he possesses by faith. (*Luther's Works*, Vol. 26, p. 89)

In short, we can stand the loss of our possessions, our name, our life, and everything else; but we will not let ourselves be deprived of the Gospel, our faith, and Jesus Christ. And that is that. Accursed be any humility that yields or submits at this point! Rather let everyone be proud and unremitting here, unless he wants to deny Christ. With the help of God, therefore, I will be more hardheaded than anyone else. I want to be stubborn and to be known as someone who is stubborn. Here I bear the inscription "I yield to no one." (*Luther's Works*, Vol. 26, p. 99)

2:11-21
Living in Line With the Gospel

The late seminary professor Dr. Siegbert Becker tells of a time in his ministry when he sat next to the bed of a dying Lutheran woman and spoke to her of her sin and God's grace, telling her "she need not fear death and the judgment because the Lord Jesus had taken her sin away." When he finished, her daughter, also a Lutheran, said, "Pastor, that's what I always tell mother too. She doesn't have to be afraid because she has never done anything wrong" (*The Word Goes On: Sermons by Dr. Siegbert W. Becker*, Milwaukee: Northwestern Publishing House, 1992, p. 130).

This daughter was surely taught repeatedly that all people are by birth and nature sinful and that we are saved by grace alone through faith alone in Christ alone. And yet out of her mouth came something that could have been said by any adherent of bad religion who thinks human good deeds will win the favor of some generic, nameless god in the unseen heavens.

This happens more often than we care to admit. Some people can spend a lifetime at the feet of Christian pastors and teachers, singing with gusto, "Nothing in my hand I bring, simply to thy cross I cling" (CW 839). They can memorize Paul's words, "It is by grace you have been saved, through faith—and this is not from yourselves, it is the gift of God—not by works, so that no one can boast" (Ephesians 2:8,9). And then in reference to some Christless relative, these lifelong Christians may say, "Well, he's such a good guy. I'm sure God will take him in." Or when getting the bad news that their own time is short, they say something like "Well, I've tried to live a good life."

Why is it that we understand with our heads in confirmation class and Bible classes when the pastor outlines the difference between law and gospel on a chalkboard—"SOS: the law shows our sin. SOS: the gospel shows our Savior"—but we have such a hard time holding on to this with our hearts? It is because there is a virus that infects our bones till the day we die. The church fathers gave this virus a Latin label: the *opinio legis*—"the opinion of the law." It is a notion we are born with: that our standing with God depends on our own doing; that we are not nearly as helpless and hopeless as the Bible says we are; that if we just try our best or jump through certain hoops, God will cut us some slack.

As baptized sons and daughters of our Father, you and I see this for the lie that it is. We know that we are saved by the doing, dying, and rising of God's Son, who rendered to God the obedience we could not give, who paid the price for sin that we could not pay, who on Easter morning scored the game point against the opponent we could never beat—death itself.

This is the beating heart of the Bible. It is the gospel, the good news that we are justified, declared righteous, and pronounced not guilty before God. And when he brings us to believe in what Christ has already done for us, this divine verdict becomes our dearest treasure. Paul's letter to the Galatian Christians is a trumpet call to believe and cherish this.

In the verses before us, we learn that while living in line with the gospel will always be perilous, it is always priceless. Whether in the age of the apostles, the age of the Reformation, or our own age of sickly secularism, living in line with the gospel is always in peril. What surprises us in Paul's account is that like that Lutheran daughter in the hospital room, the best of us can fail to live out what we say we believe.

¹¹But when Cephas came to Antioch, I opposed him to his face, because he was clearly wrong. ¹²For before some people came from James, he ate with the Gentiles. But when those people came, he drew back and separated himself, because he feared those from the circumcision group. ¹³And the rest of the Jews joined him in his hypocrisy, with the result that even Barnabas was carried away by their hypocrisy. ¹⁴But when I saw that they were not acting according to the truth of the gospel, I said to Cephas in front of all of them, "If you, a Jew, live like the Gentiles and not like the Jews, why do you compel the Gentiles to live like the Jews?"

Paul here calls Peter by his Aramaic name, Cephas. Not long after that meeting in Jerusalem where all the apostles were on the same page about their gospel freedom, Peter pays a visit to the church in Syrian Antioch. This congregation was the home base for Paul and his traveling coworkers. It was from Antioch that Paul set out on his various missionary journeys. The congregation there was populated with both Jews and Gentiles who had been brought to believe in Jesus as their Savior. The issues of circumcision and eating ceremonially unclean foods had long been settled for them. They comfortably mingled with one another. They respected one another's liberty and scruples without passing judgment. Peter himself hung out with the gentile believers, unafraid to eat with them, maybe even sharing a ceremonially unclean pork chop or ham sandwich. Peter was living in line with the gospel.

But now some believing Jews come to Antioch "from James." This does not necessarily mean that James, the brother of the Lord, sent them. The church in Jerusalem was so identified with James as its head that this may simply mean these Jews came from Jerusalem. James had already expressed his agreement with Peter and Paul on the matter of gospel liberty. We are not even told that the believing Jews from Jerusalem cause any trouble at this time. But their very presence spooks Peter. He suddenly becomes paranoid about the whole issue of eating with the Gentiles. Is he afraid of criticism? Does he fear that it might cause trouble?

Whatever it is, Peter noticeably pulls back from eating with the gentile believers. And because Peter is one of the pillars of the early church, the other Jews in Antioch follow his lead. Even Paul's mission partner Barnabas is led astray by the hypocrisy.

It's not so much a matter of what Peter eats or doesn't eat. Paul himself conducted himself differently at different times. He said to the Corinthians, "To the Jews, I became like a Jew so that I might gain Jews. . . . To those who are without the law, I became like a person without the law. . . . I have become all things to all people so that I may save at least some" (1 Corinthians 9:20-22). The wrong thing here is that Peter sends the definite signal to both the Jews and Gentiles in the church at Antioch that the Gentiles are perhaps second-class Christians, that perhaps it is necessary after all to keep the laws of Moses to gain God's favor, that perhaps faith in Christ is not enough.

The wrong thing—and Paul uses the word twice—is the *hypocrisy* of what Peter is doing. This word, in the language of the New Testament, literally means one who plays a part or wears a mask—you know, an actor. Actors pretend to be what they are not. Hypocrites play a role; they play a part. Peter and those who follow his lead act as though they believe something that they do not. They are not living in line with the gospel they preach.

Paul sees that this conduct is not in step with the truth of the gospel. He confronts Peter to his face, not talk behind his back. It is a public thing that must be handled publicly. Paul calls Peter on the carpet for this in front of the people. It isn't that Peter fails to know and preach the pure gospel. It isn't that Peter is any less of an apostle when he picks up his pen to write his inspired epistles. But Peter is just as much flesh and blood as the rest of us are. His fear of what people think is getting the best of him. He may talk the talk, but he is not walking the walk in line with the gospel. Others are also being led astray. Living in line with the gospel is always in peril in every age.

We have seen this in Peter before: brave one second and timid the next—daring to walk to Jesus on the water one minute, in over his head next; swearing up and down that he will never deny Jesus, swearing only hours later that he has never met Jesus. Peter battled the same demons over and over in his life. So do you, and so do I. It is the devil's *modus operandi*, the way he works, wearing us down with the same old weaknesses. Peter knows this. He humbly accepts the rebuke. It has been a momentary lapse.

On this point Luther remarks that David, Samson, and many other heroes of faith who were full of the Holy Spirit also fell into huge sins. Job and Jeremiah cursed the day of their birth. Elijah and Jonah grew tired of life and prayed for death. The Bible paints these believers with warts and all so when we are troubled, we may find comfort, and when we are proud, we may take warning. No one has ever fallen so badly that he or she may not stand up again by God's grace. No one has such a sure footing that he or she cannot fall. If Peter fell, I too could fall. If he stood up again, so can I.

Paul does not assume an air of superiority over Peter. He uses the word *we* when he points out that living in line with the gospel is always priceless.

> [15]"We are Jews by birth and not Gentile sinners. [16]We know that a person is not justified by the works of the law but through faith in Jesus Christ. So we also believed in Christ Jesus that we might be justified by faith in Christ and not by the works of the law, because no one will be justified by the works of the law. [17]But if, while seeking to be justified in Christ, we ourselves were also found to be sinners, then is Christ a servant of sin? Certainly not!
>
> [18]"In fact, if I build up again those things that I destroyed, I bring on myself the judgment of being a lawbreaker. [19]Indeed, through the law I died to the law that I might live for God. [20]I have been crucified with Christ, and I no longer live, but Christ lives in me. The life I am now living in the flesh, I live by faith in the Son of God, who loved me and gave himself for me. [21]I do not regard the grace of God as nothing. As a matter of fact, if righteousness is through the law, then Christ died for nothing!"

"The truth of the gospel is just this," says Paul, "whether Jew or Gentile, we are justified not by works of the law but through faith in Jesus Christ, because by works of the law no one will be justified."

"Now," says Paul, "if in this endeavor to be justified by faith in Christ we Jewish Christians become just like those gentile sinners by no longer observing the law, does that mean Christ is a servant of sin, promoting disobedience to God? Certainly not! The real sin would be to pretend Christ never fulfilled the law. The real sin would be to rebuild these ceremonial laws that merely pointed ahead to Christ. Through the law, I died to the law, that is, I have nothing to do with the law as a way to become right with God. I saw that I couldn't keep it at all ... so then the only way to live was to trust in Christ. If this is not so, then Christ died for nothing.

"Here is what is priceless: I have been crucified with Christ. His death for sin is now my death for sin. His payment is my payment. His righteousness is my righteousness. All that belongs to Christ—yes, his victory over the grave too—is now mine by faith. Now this life that I live in the flesh on this side of heaven—it's no longer I who live but Christ who is living in me. My former lifestyle, focused on obeying the law and failing, gave way to a new life empowered by Christ and enjoying forgiveness.

"Living in line with the gospel is always priceless. For 'the life I am now living in the flesh, I live by faith in the Son of God, who loved me and gave himself for me.' "

See how personal this is for Paul. Write in your own name here too. It is easy enough to say, "All have sinned." It is another thing to confess, "*I* am a sinner." It is one thing to glibly say, "We all have to go sometime." It is another thing to say, "*I* must die." It is one thing to speculate, "Judgment day is coming." It is another thing to remember, "*I* must appear before the throne of Christ." It is also one thing to say, "Jesus died for all." This is true! But I am part of that "all." It is a priceless thing to believe and say with Paul, "The Son of God, who loved *me* [even before there was a me] and gave himself for *me*." Shall this not make me a different me than I was?

Lines From Luther

> He [Paul] does not attack Peter sharply; he treats
> him with due respect. But because he sees that the pres-
> tige of Peter is endangering the majesty of the doctrine

of justification, he ignores the prestige, in order to keep this doctrine pure and undefiled. (*Luther's Works*, Vol. 26, p. 106)

The apostles were not superior to us in anything except in their apostolic office. We have the same gifts that they had, namely, the same Christ, Baptism, Word, and forgiveness of sins. They needed all this no less than we do; they were sanctified and saved by all this just as we are. (*Luther's Works*, Vol. 26, p. 109)

It is truly amazing that such great men as Peter, Barnabas, and the others fell so quickly and easily, especially in the matter of a work which they knew to be good and they themselves had previously taught to others. . . . Therefore we are nothing, even with all our great gifts, unless God is present. When He deserts us and leaves us to our own resources, our wisdom and knowledge are nothing. Unless He sustains us continually, the highest learning and even theology are useless. For in the hour of temptation it can suddenly happen that by a trick of the devil all the comforting texts disappear from our sight and only the threatening ones appear to overwhelm us. (*Luther's Works*, Vol. 26, p. 114)

Therefore whoever knows well how to distinguish the Gospel from the Law should give thanks to God and know that he is a real theologian. (*Luther's Works*, Vol. 26, p. 115)

Therefore let everyone learn diligently how to distinguish the Law from the Gospel, not only in words but in feeling and in experience; that is, let him distinguish well between these two in his heart and in his conscience. For so far as the words are concerned, the distinction is easy. But when it comes to experience, you will find the Gospel a rare guest but the Law a constant guest in your conscience, which is habituated to the Law and the sense of sin; reason, too, supports this sense. (*Luther's Works*, Vol. 26, p. 117)

Therefore when the Law terrifies you, sin accuses you, and your conscience is crushed, you must say: "There is a time to die and a time to live" (Eccl. 3:2). There is a time to hear the Law and a time to despise the Law. There is a time to hear the Gospel and a time to know nothing about the Gospel. . . . Thus the Law remains in the valley with the ass, and the Gospel remains with Isaac on the mountain. (*Luther's Works*, Vol. 26, p. 117)

Then there comes, at the appropriate time, the saving Word of the Gospel, which says: "Take heart, my son; your sins are forgiven (Matt. 9:2). Believe in Jesus Christ, who was crucified for your sins. If you feel your sins, do not consider them in yourself but remember that they have been transferred to Christ, 'with whose stripes you are healed' (Is. 53:3)." (*Luther's Works*, Vol. 26, pp. 131,132)

Therefore we define a Christian as follows: A Christian is not someone who has no sin or feels no sin; he is someone to whom, because of his faith in Christ, God does not impute his sin. This doctrine brings firm consolation to troubled consciences amid genuine terrors. (*Luther's Works*, Vol. 26, p. 133)

3:1-14
The Road to Spiritual Renewal

It was Jesus who told us that the love of most would grow cold (Matthew 24:12). It was Jesus who told the people of the church at Ephesus that they had forsaken their first love (Revelation 2:4). It was Jesus who told the people of the church at Laodicea that they were neither hot nor cold but lukewarm, and so he would spit them out of his mouth (Revelation 3:15,16).

The virus of spiritual backsliding appears in every age. Ours too. We grieve over the symptoms when we see them in ourselves and others. The symptoms are not so much seen in those who openly throw away the gift of the gospel and go to hell honestly. The symptoms are more likely among those who wrap the gospel and the faith that goes with it in a nice hanky and bury them in a hole as a little insurance policy. The symptoms are seen in those who want to hang on to heaven with one hand and keep a few grubby souvenirs of hell in the other. It is like hanging on to your official church membership but not showing up for Word and sacrament. Or singing some Christmas carols but politely telling Jesus where to get off when it comes to your cussing, boozing, or immoral sexual habits.

The symptoms of backsliding are not only in others and not always visibly dramatic, but we also sense them in ourselves. Our walk with God is weak. Our prayer life gets animated only when we need a fire extinguisher. Our appetite for God's Word fades. Jesus is demoted to being an hors d'oeuvre, not the main course.

We sense something is dreadfully wrong, something that cannot be fixed with more campaigns or gimmickry, more church volunteerism or loud denominational "rah-rah." We sense we are wandering from home. We wonder about the road back to our Father, the path to spiritual renewal.

There are lots of voices offering directions. These voices often portray salvation as a minor repair job rather than a rescue story. They pay lip service to the cross and empty tomb but trade away their transforming power for a litany of laws, steps, and principles expressing structured plans to overcome sinful habits—leading souls to either self-righteous pharisaism or hopeless despair. These voices serenade us with a tune of self-help and self-interest, garnished with a few Bible passages. These "other gospels" appeal to our human nature, for they ultimately make us the central focus instead of Christ. These "other gospels" are imitation solutions peddled by impostor evangelists.

The impostors seem like smiling angels of light when they walk in the door of the Galatian congregations founded by Paul. They offer a fuller gospel and holier feeling by going back to circumcision, dietary rules, and other ceremonial laws of Moses, which Christ already fulfilled by his coming. The Galatians are buying the concoction these Judaizers are selling. Here, they think, is the road to real spiritual renewal.

But the Galatians are looking primarily at their own doing instead of at Christ's doing. They are treating the symptoms with the law instead of treating the virus with the gospel. They are taking a dangerous detour instead of the real road home. Here in the lines of Paul's urgent letter to his beloved Galatians stands the apostle at the crossroads, pointing out the real road to spiritual renewal. He will seek to demonstrate the trustworthiness of this road by appealing to their own experience, citing the example of the patriarch Abraham, exposing the unthinkable alternative, and highlighting what Christ has already done.

While Paul is founding a congregation in Corinth, the Judaizers grab their chance in Galatia. Like pied pipers, they dance the Galatians down a detour. The signpost says, "Unless you are circumcised according to the law handed down by Moses, you cannot be saved" (Acts 15:1). Paul rebukes this error with a fatherly reminder to the Galatians that the real road to spiritual renewal is obvious from their own experience.

3:1O foolish Galatians, who has bewitched you? Before your very eyes Jesus Christ was clearly portrayed as crucified. 2I just want to learn this from you: Did you receive the Spirit by the works of the law, or by believing what you heard?

3Are you so foolish? Having begun by the Spirit, are you now trying to reach the goal by the flesh? 4Did you experience so many things for nothing, if it were indeed for nothing? 5So then, does the one who supplies the Spirit to you and works miracles among you, do it by the works of the law? Or does he do it by your believing what you hear?

The frustrated father asks his child, "What's gotten into you?" The frustrated apostle asks, "O foolish Galatians! Who has bewitched you? This isn't what you learned from me. Before your very eyes Jesus Christ was clearly portrayed as crucified."

Can you hear him talking to us? "From the time you were carried to the baptismal font and in your home, church, and Sunday school, Jesus Christ has been held in front of you like a big billboard in bold colors as the God-man—born, crucified, risen, and returning. It has always been Christ's work, not our work—Christ instead of us, for us, in place of us. Faith in him has always been the only road home to God. Now you are tired of the old gospel, your solid but simple Christianity. You hanker after something more practical, doable. Christ is no longer enough."

Paul is saying, "My dear Galatians, I am not writing you off or giving up on you. I know how slick these new salespeople sound to you. But just one question: How did you receive the Holy Spirit and become new spiritual creatures in Christ Jesus? Was it by obeying the law or believing the good news that you heard? You know the answer, don't you? The chains fell from your hearts and darkness surrendered to light in your souls *not* when you did enough, paid enough, or suffered enough but when you heard that *Christ* did enough, paid enough, and suffered enough.

"Now are you so foolish that having begun by the Spirit, having begun the journey by faith in Christ, that you now want to switch horses in the middle of the road and get lost down some other path? Having been *drawn* by the sweet gospel, do you now want to be *driven* by 'Six Secrets to Friendship With God,' 'Five Attitudes of Real Servants,' or endless sets of *shoulds* and *oughts*? Do you imagine you can be perfected, reach the goal, and get the rest of the way home by the sinful flesh, by personal obedience to the law? Did you suffer so many bad things for the gospel and experience so many good things in vain, all for nothing?

"Oh, I haven't given up on you. Maybe it wasn't for nothing! Think of the God who supplies his Spirit to you, who holds your heart in his hand when you are sad, who lifts you up when you are downhearted, and who listens to your prayers and does wonders in your life. Does he do all this because you earned it, or rather, as you believe him when he tells you that he sent his only Son to save you? Haven't the real blessings in your life come when you simply take God at his word? You know the real road to spiritual renewal in your own life. It's obvious from your own experience!"

The real road to spiritual renewal is obvious also from the example of Abraham that Paul now highlights.

> **⁶In the same way as Abraham "believed God, and it was credited to him as righteousness." ⁷Understand, then, that those who believe are the children of Abraham. ⁸Foreseeing that God would justify the Gentiles by faith, Scripture proclaimed the gospel in advance to Abraham, saying, "In you, all nations will be blessed." ⁹So then, those who have faith are blessed along with Abraham, the man of faith.**

Paul uses a case history to make his point. That's because a picture is worth a thousand words. We see this often on the pages of the Scriptures. Jesus doesn't merely say, "Love your neighbor." He paints the picture with the parable of the Good Samaritan (Luke 10:25-37). Jesus not only tells us that God is a gracious Father who waits for his wayward children to come home again, but he also tells us the parable of the Prodigal Son, who gets up from the pigsty of his rebellion in a far country and goes home to find a forgiving father (Luke 15:11-32).

The Scriptures present real case histories as well. The Scriptures not only tell us, "An eye that mocks its father and despises the obedience due its mother—ravens of the valley will peck it out, and young vultures will eat it" (Proverbs 30:17), but they also record the case history of David's rebellious son, Absalom, and the silent heap of stones in the forest of Ephraim where that young man's body was thrown after his failed bid to steal the kingdom from his father (2 Samuel 18:17). The Bible not only tells us that God will be with us when we walk through the fires of trouble (Isaiah 43:2), but it also tells us of those three Hebrew models of faithfulness who were actually thrown into a fiery furnace and were then delivered by God (Daniel 3:8-30).

So here also Paul calls to mind the case history of Abraham set down on the pages of Genesis. The Bible says that God called Abraham to forsake country and kindred—to leave behind a civilization that archaeologists tell us had fine homes, libraries, and, yes, indoor plumbing—to go to a land of unfamiliar and often unfriendly faces, to live a life of a wandering nomad in dusty tents. God "proclaimed the gospel in advance to Abraham," says Paul. God gave Abraham a cluster of promises—about becoming a great nation, being blessed, and being a blessing to all the world (Genesis 12:1-3). To the Jews and Gentiles, to the Galatians, and to you and me too, God promised blessings through the birth of a promised son, a son through whom would come the Savior of the world.

God talked with Abraham many times during his lifetime and did so in a variety of ways. He appeared to Abraham in a mystical vision of a smoking firepot, a blazing torch, and deep darkness (Genesis 15:17). When Abraham was 99 years old, God appeared to him in human form and had lunch in the shade of a tree outside Abraham's tent (Genesis 18:8). And the promise of a son was repeated.

But despite the revelations and conversations, there were long years of bewildering silence. There was nothing but the promise of God to cling to. What were Abraham and Sarah tempted to think? That God had dangled the promise of a child in front of them and was now sitting on his hands and watching as they both advanced toward tottering old age? What kind of game was that? What did God want?

God wanted faith. God created that faith in Abraham's heart. The Bible says—and Paul repeats it to the Galatians—"Abraham 'believed God, and it was credited to him as righteousness.' " By faith, Abraham laid hold of a righteousness earned for him by a coming Savior. "Abraham was glad that he would see my day. He saw it and rejoiced," said the Savior Jesus, who went on to say, "Before Abraham was born, I am" (John 8:56,58). Abraham knew the real road to spiritual renewal. It had nothing to do with him and everything to do with Christ.

The road to spiritual renewal is also obvious from the unthinkable alternative that now becomes Paul's focus.

[10]**In fact, those who rely on the works of the law are under a curse. For it is written, "Cursed is everyone who does not continue to do everything written in the book of the law."** [11]**Clearly no one is declared righteous before God by the law, because "The righteous will live by faith."** [12]**The law does not say "by faith." Instead it says, "The one who does these things will live by them."**

"Listen, my beloved Galatians," says Paul, "you know what I taught you. The Bible has two primary teachings: the law and the gospel. The law is not a bad message or a wrong word. It is a holy message, God's Word. But it is not a *saving* word. And the reason is found in us, not in the content of the law. Sinners from birth that we are, we can't keep it."

The law plays fair and square: eternal life for those who keep it and eternal damnation for those who break it. The law pronounces a curse on everyone who does not fully obey it, who does not continually do the things written in it. If you want to be saved by the law, you have to keep all of it, not some of it. You have to keep it perfectly, not partially. You have to keep it all the time, not just some of the time.

Care to try? Do you really want to tell Christ that your obedience is as good as his, that your payment is sufficient like his, that your own efforts avail before God? Are you your own savior?

The guilt of sin can be in only one of two places—either on Christ or on you. Which will it be? The real road to spiritual renewal, to a right relationship with God, is obvious when you compare these two alternatives, isn't it? The road to spiritual renewal is obvious from what Christ has already done.

> [13]**Christ redeemed us from the curse of the law by becoming a curse for us. As it is written, "Cursed is everyone who hangs on a tree." [14]He redeemed us in order that the blessing of Abraham would come to the Gentiles through Christ Jesus, so that we would receive the promised Spirit through faith.**

Criminals were hanged on a tree, crucified. So says Deuteronomy 21:23 as quoted by Paul, "Cursed is everyone who is hanged on a tree." Christ was hanged on the tree of the cross. He redeemed us—ransomed us when we were held hostage by sin, death, and hell—by becoming a curse for us, in our place, in our stead, so that we might receive the promised Spirit through faith. You and I will never have to wonder whether we have done enough. It doesn't depend on whether we have done enough. We never can. We never will. Christ has done enough.

Jesus told Nicodemus that the road to spiritual renewal for dead hearts was as simple as Moses lifting up the serpent in the wilderness so that everyone who looked to it was healed (John 3:14).

And the serpent, the appointed instrument of salvation, had the appearance of the curse! Everyone who looks to the Savior who was cursed and lynched on the tree of the cross in our stead has eternal life—a new kind of life. Such a person is born again, born from above. To the Galatians, to you and me, Jesus says, "I who had no sin became sin for you so that you might become the righteousness of God in me. I did for you what you could not do, died for you so that you might not die, rose for you so that you might live for me and with me forever. .

"Don't go off road, my child. I am the Way, for any other way will get you lost. I am the Truth, no matter how you feel on any given morning when you get up to face a world of lies. I am the Life, even when you go to bed feeling defeated by the day's events." As one hymn writer put it, "I cling to what my Savior taught and trust it, whether felt or not" (*Evangelical Lutheran Hymnary*, hymn 226:10). Now let no one bewitch you!

Lines From Luther

Therefore faith alone attributes glory to God. Paul testifies to this in the case of Abraham in Rom. 4:20, when he says: "Abraham grew strong in faith as he gave glory to God." And he adds from Gen. 15:6 that this was imputed to him as righteousness. (*Luther's Works*, Vol. 26, p. 229)

We, on the other hand, teach and comfort an afflicted sinner this way: "Brother, it is impossible for you to become so righteous in this life that your body is as clear and spotless as the sun. You still have spots and wrinkles (Eph. 5:27), and yet you are holy." But you say: "How can I be holy when I have sin and am aware of it?" "That you feel and acknowledge sin—this is good. Thank God, and do not despair. It is one step toward health when a sick man admits and confesses his disease." "But how will I be liberated from sin?" "Run to Christ, the Physician, who heals the contrite of heart and saves sinners. Believe in Him. If you believe, you are righteous, because you attribute to God the glory of being almighty, merciful, truthful, etc. You justify and praise God. In short, you attribute divinity and everything to Him. And the sin that still remains in you is not imputed but is forgiven for the sake of Christ, in whom you believe and who is perfectly righteous in a formal sense. His righteousness is yours; your sin is His." (*Luther's Works*, Vol. 26, p. 233)

Who will reconcile those utterly conflicting statements, that the sin in us is not sin, that he who is damnable will not be damned, that he who is rejected will not be rejected, that he who is worthy of wrath and eternal death will not receive these punishments? Only the Mediator between God and man, Jesus Christ (1 Tim. 2:5). As Paul says, "there is no condemnation for those who are in Christ Jesus." (*Luther's Works*, Vol. 26, pp. 235,236)

From this it follows that the blessing and the faith of Abraham are the same as ours, that Abraham's Christ is our Christ, and that Christ died for Abraham's sins as well as for ours. John 8:56: "Abraham saw My day and was glad." (*Luther's Works*, Vol. 26, p. 244)

Whatever sins I, you, and all of us have committed or may commit in the future, they are as much Christ's own as if He Himself had committed them. In short, our sin must be Christ's own sin, or we shall perish eternally. (*Luther's Works*, Vol. 26, p. 278)

This is the most joyous of all doctrines and the one that contains the most comfort. It teaches that we have the indescribable and inestimable mercy and love of God. When the merciful Father saw that we were being oppressed through the Law, that we were being held under a curse, and that we could not be liberated from it by anything, He sent His Son into the world, heaped all the sins of all men upon Him, and said to Him: "Be Peter the denier; Paul the persecutor, blasphemer, and assaulter; David the adulterer; the sinner who ate the apple in Paradise; the thief on the cross. In short, be the person of all men, the one who has committed the sins of all men. And see to it that You pay and make satisfaction for them." (*Luther's Works*, Vol. 26, p. 280)

By this deed the whole world is purged and expiated from all sins, and thus it is set free from death and from every evil. (*Luther's Works*, Vol. 26, p. 280)

If the sins of the entire world are on that one man, Jesus Christ, then they are not on the world. . . . Not only my sins and yours, but the sins of the entire world, past, present, and future, attack Him, try to damn Him, and do in fact damn Him. . . . Thus in Christ all sin is conquered, killed and buried; and righteousness remains the victor and the ruler eternally. (*Luther's Works*, Vol. 26, pp. 280,281)

Therefore the one and only way to avoid the curse is to believe and to say with sure confidence: "Thou, O Christ, art my sin and my curse;" or rather: "I am Thy sin, Thy curse, Thy death, Thy wrath of God, Thy hell. But Thou art my Righteousness, Blessing, Life, Grace of God, and Heaven." For the text clearly states: "Christ became a curse for us." Therefore we are the reason why He became a curse; indeed, we are His curse. (*Luther's Works*, Vol. 26, pp. 291,292)

3:15-25

What a Deal!

"Let's make a deal!" That's the way most folks see their relationship with God, if they care to have one at all. We're born with this opinion of the law, as our teachers consistently called it, this notion that if we do a little better and try a little harder, we can contribute at least something to gain a right relationship with God.

This opinion of the law is the bread and butter of every non-Christian religion. Many think of biblical Christianity as merely one out of a hundred or thousand other religions. But there are really only two religions in the whole world and all of history. There is the religion of works, an obedience to rules or laws. And there is the religion of grace, God's undeserved love in Christ.

Whatever else one might say about Islam, Buddhism, Hinduism, the cults of the Jehovah's Witnesses or Mormons, or the Freemasons' Great Architect of the Universe, this much they all have in common: They are all religions of the law, based to some degree on human doing rather than entirely on the doing, dying, and rising of our atoning Savior and Substitute Jesus Christ. Without exception they hiss into human hearts the lethal lie with which the old serpent enticed Eve in the beginning: that we can be like God, that we can in fact become gods of our own lives and contribute something to save ourselves.

Our Sunday school children know better. For them it is as simple as Jesus' own words in John 3:16: "For God so loved the world that he gave his only-begotten Son, that whoever believes in him shall not perish, but have eternal life."

Our catechism students know better. They memorize Paul's words: "It is by grace you have been saved, through faith—and this is not from yourselves, it is the gift of God—not by works, so that no one can boast" (Ephesians 2:8,9).

You and I know better. The gospel is the good news of an infinitely better deal God has to offer us—a deal that requires nothing on our part and everything on his part; a deal with no small print at the bottom of the page, no money down, no deferred payments, and no hidden fees. What a deal!

In fact, it's such an amazing deal that even we who have heard it all our lives keep scanning the deal for the small print. Our sinful nature asks, "What's the catch?" or suggests the cliché, "If it sounds too good to be true, it probably is." After all, there are no free lunches. We live in a world of wheelers and dealers and movers and shakers. On every other human level, from academics to athletics, from childcare to careers, we get out of it what we put into it, right? Why should it be any different when it comes to our standing with God?

In Paul's day, the Judaizers appeal to the opinion of the law in the hearts of the Galatian Christians. They offer a different kind of deal, a different and diluted gospel. The deal says, "Yes, believe in Jesus, but unless you keep God's Old Testament deal with the ancient Israelites, the covenant deal of circumcision, ceremonial laws, dietary rules, etc., you cannot be saved." Paul fires off this letter to the Galatians to remind them of the deal God has given them. It is the only and original deal by which we are saved, and it is the primary deal of grace for which the law is only preparatory.

Taking aim at the Judaizers, Paul points out this unique gospel deal of grace by which we are saved.

> [15]**Brothers, I am speaking in human terms. When someone has established a last will and testament, no one nullifies it or adds to it.** [16]**The promises God spoke referred to Abraham and to his seed. It doesn't say, "And to seeds," as if it were referring to many, but, as referring to one, "And to your seed," who is Christ.** [17]**What I am saying is this: The law, which came into being 430 years after the covenant established earlier by God in Christ, does not annul that covenant, with the result that it invalidates the promise.** [18]**In fact, if the inheritance is by the law, it is no longer by the promise. But God graciously gave it to Abraham by a promise.**

There was indeed a law deal that God gave to his Old Testament people. It was a two-way agreement God made with the Israelites at Mount Sinai. If they obeyed his code of civil, ceremonial, and moral laws that set them apart as his special nation, he would shower them with earthly blessings. They agreed. "Everything that the LORD has said, we will do," they loudly shouted at the foot of the mountain (Exodus 19:8). This law code is sometimes called the Law of Moses, because the Lord used Moses as the messenger or mediator while revealing the covenant to the nation of Israel.

But this law deal at Mount Sinai had an expiration date stamped on it. It was temporary and time sensitive. It was never intended to save anyone. The original deal, God's gospel covenant, went back much further than the Law of Moses. From the time God promised Adam and Eve a Savior who would crush the serpent's head (Genesis 3:15), this covenant, this will and testament, was the real deal and the only deal for all of humanity.

"Let me illustrate," says Paul. "When someone has established a last will and testament, no one nullifies it or adds to it." This expression that Paul uses, "last will and testament," is sometimes translated "covenant." Jesus used the expression when he said, "This is my blood of the new testament [or new covenant]," while instituting the Lord's Supper.

Luther remarks that a testament is made by someone who expects to die, and a covenant or promise is made by someone who expects to continue living. In Holy Communion, through the very body and blood of Christ, we are pointed to the last will and testament of our Savior, the God-man who died so we might inherit forgiveness and life eternal. But we also have the covenant of the God who intended to live and rose from the dead to give us a place at his heavenly table. So in this one little word—*diatheke* in Greek, "testament/covenant" in English—is the teaching that Christ died and rose again.

"When someone has established a last will and testament, no one nullifies it or adds to it." If you legally and properly will your brother-in-law $50,000, and then he runs off to Las Vegas with your wife, you can't simply run to the cedar chest, pull out the will, run a big red line through his name, and say, "Nuts to you!" No, you would have to jump through all the proper legal hoops to change a will or covenant even on a human level.

"Now," says Paul, "how much truer is this in the case of God's original gospel deal?" God affirmed and formalized his gospel promise of grace to Abraham. God gave this gospel deal to Abraham in reference to his seed, that is, his offspring. God was not merely using a collective plural as in "seeds" or "offsprings." He was also referring to only one seed or offspring—the coming Christ. Paul is not necessarily saying that the promises to Abraham (as in Genesis 22:18) had nothing to do with the rest of his descendants but that the primary focus of and essential key to those promises was one singular offspring: Jesus Christ. The temporary deal or covenant at Mount Sinai didn't come for another 430 years. This code of Moses did not nullify the only and original deal by which we are saved. In fact, if the inheritance is by the law, it is no longer by the promise. But God graciously gave this inheritance to Abraham by a promise. The original covenant of grace precedes and supersedes the temporary covenant of Mount Sinai.

"These Judaizers," says Paul, "are offering you Galatians something temporary for something eternal. They are pointing you to your own doing of the law instead of to the done deal of Christ who lived, died, and rose again in your stead and on your behalf."

Paul explains further. This gospel promise is the primary deal of grace for which the law is only preparatory.

¹⁹**Then what about the law? It was added for the purpose of revealing transgressions, until the Seed to whom the promise referred had come. It was transmitted through angels by the hand of a mediator. ²⁰Now a mediator is not needed for one party, but God is one.**

Paul anticipates a question: Then what about the law? If we are saved by grace alone as it was promised to Abraham, then what is with all the thunder and lightning of Mount Sinai? What is with all those Old Testament ceremonial laws given to the Israelites?

"It was added for the purpose of revealing transgressions," says Paul, "until the Seed to whom the promise referred had come," namely, Christ. It was preparatory. It placed sin under a magnifying glass so that people could see sin for what it is and know very well their utter inability to keep the law. It magnified their infinite need of the *real* deal, the *primary* deal: a Savior.

"If you really think the law is the way to be saved," says Paul to the confused Galatian Christians, "remember that not even the people of Israel liked the law or wanted to deal with it." Amid the smoke and fire, the thunder and lightning, the trumpet blasts of angels and the voice of God in their ears, they scattered and ran. They pleaded for Moses to serve as an intermediary: "Speak with us yourself, and we will listen, but do not let God speak with us, or we will die" (Exodus 20:19). Divine law is directed at flawed creatures, human beings. This highlights the importance of an intermediary. The gospel is all about the one God who became one of us to offer us the real deal of grace with himself as the mediator.

Paul clarifies the preparatory nature of the law in another way.

> **²¹Then is the law against the promises of God? Certainly not! For if there had been a law given that could give life, certainly righteousness would have been derived from the law. ²²But Scripture imprisoned all things under sin, so that the promise by faith in Jesus Christ would be given to those who believe. ²³But before this faith came, we were held in custody under the law, imprisoned until the coming faith was revealed.**

The law imprisons us under sin. Its purpose is not to impart life to sinners but to declare us guilty and send us off to the dungeon so that all of us, Jew and Gentile alike, might see our helplessness and then be led to rely on the promise received by faith in Jesus Christ.

The laws of Moses to which the Judaizers want the Galatians to return were never meant to save anyone. The believers of the Old Testament, all of them, were saved the same way you and I are saved—through faith in Christ. They believed in the Christ who was coming. We believe in the Christ who has come.

The law was a temporary device of outward discipline. It kept the Israelites separate and in line until the coming of Christ. Here's the neat picture Paul uses to make his point.

> **[24]So the law was our chaperone until Christ, so that we might be justified by faith. [25]But now that this faith has come, we are no longer under a chaperone.**

The Law of Moses was not a Savior for the Israelites. It was a chaperone, a guardian, until Christ came. There is a fascinating picture in the word Paul uses here for "chaperone." It takes us back to the Greek world in which Paul lived. He is talking about a person called a *paidagogos*. This person was typically, in the strict sense, a slave, but was usually of very superior caliber and well educated. Think of the British butler on the TV series *Family Affair* from years ago—Mr. French—who ends up taking care of two little kids, Jody and Buffy. The sophisticated man played the role of a guardian, a male nanny, a chaperone.

In Paul's day, a *paidagogos* usually had charge of a boy from the age of 6 to about 16. This chaperone, male nanny, or guardian made the boy toe the line in all the details of his young life—eating properly, dressing well, minding his manners, getting along on the playground, going to school, and learning his lessons. The temporary guardian controlled the boy's every movement.

None of this made the guardian the child's father. The boy was already his father's child and heir of the whole estate before the *paidagogos* came along. The boy would continue to be his father's child and heir of everything long after his childhood guardian was gone.

Paul says the Law of Moses was the Israelites' *paidagogos*, their chaperone or guardian until Christ came. God was dealing with the Israelites as immature children, not yet ready for the full freedom of adulthood. The law did not change who they were: children of their heavenly Father. This law chaperone could not take away the inheritance that was theirs through the promise of the coming Savior given to Abraham.

And once the Israelites had grown up, once Christ finally came, the job of the chaperone, that code of Moses, would be done. Believers would no longer need the rules and regulations of this babysitter to prepare them for life in Christ.

What Paul says to the Galatians he says to you and me. What a deal God has given us! It is the only and original deal by which we are saved. It is the primary deal of grace for which the law is only preparatory. Even now, the unchanging moral will of God, expressed in parts of the Sinai law code, gets us ready for Christ. It plows up the ground of our hearts so we might receive the seed of the gospel. It shows us our sin that we might receive the gospel. It makes us hungry for the Bread of Life.

The Lord once shared with the suffering Job, "Who has the wisdom to count the clouds and to empty the water jars of the sky, when the loose dust has been poured into molds to harden, and the clods of dirt are cemented together?" (Job 38:37,38). God alone has the wisdom to "empty the water jars of the sky" at just the right time. Similarly, even the dry spells and droughts have their purpose in our lives. When the sunbaked fields are dry enough, the clods of earth stick together, and the ground cracks and opens its thirsty throat to receive the rain. When our consciences are stricken by divine law, in love and wisdom God delights to quench our spiritual thirst with the unconditional gospel.

So when we see ourselves as the barren wastelands that we are without Christ, when the law has cracked the soil of our hearts and we can do nothing but wait for his streams in the desert, then the heavens open, the showers of the gospel descend, we sigh with relief, and the fields of our hearts spring up to eternal life. What a deal!

Lines From Luther

If I define the Law with a proper definition and keep it in its own function and use, it is a very good thing. But if I transfer it to another use and attribute to it what should not be attributed to it, I distort not only the Law but all theology. (*Luther's Works*, Vol. 26, p. 307)

Thus it [the Law] makes us ready for Christ. He who has never tasted the bitter will not remember the sweet; hunger is the best cook. As the dry earth thirsts for rain, so the Law makes the troubled heart thirst for Christ. To such hearts Christ tastes sweetest; to them He is joy, comfort, and life. Only then are Christ and His work understood correctly. (*Luther's Works*, Vol. 26, p. 329)

GALATIANS

3:26–4:7
We've Never Had It So Good!

Here are a few things your parents said to you that you vowed you would never say to your children: "We'll see. Maybe later," "Shut the door; were you born in a barn?" "Just wait till your father gets home," "I suppose if everyone else jumped off the bridge, you would too," "You're going to poke someone's eye out with that," or the all-time favorite, "Because I said so."

But then you grew up, got married, had kids, and discovered that these profound sayings are actually hereditary. It's like you couldn't help saying the same things to your children. You discovered something else, namely, that at least some of these things are true. Take, for instance, your parents' reminder, "You've never had it so good!" Forget for a moment all the jokes about your parents walking to school barefoot, in the snow, uphill, both ways, while beating off a grizzly bear with their school textbook. When it comes to educational opportunities, technological toys, and modern conveniences, many of us have never had it so good.

Sadly, on other levels, our parents may have had it better. At least our parents knew that marriage was something between a man and a woman, that marriage was what you established *before* you moved in together, and that children were expected to obey their parents and not the other way around. So even the remark "You've never had it so good!" is only partly true part of the time.

But when it comes to every generation of believers in Christ, it is entirely true all of the time that we've never had it so good.

The believers in Galatia to whom Paul penned these lines are not so sure about that. Some false teachers, the Judaizers, have been romancing them back to the good old days, enticing them to wax nostalgic about the ceremonial laws of Moses that had been fulfilled by Christ. The song and dance of the Judaizers is that faith in Christ is fine but not enough, that the ceremonial laws of Moses are also necessary for salvation, and that the Gentiles must first become Jews to have a place in the Father's house.

Paul has been dicing this false doctrine into itsy-bitsy pieces in this letter to the Galatians. In the previous verses he says that the Law of Moses that God gave to the Israelites was like a chaperone, a guardian—Paul called it a *paidagogos*—to escort them until the promised Savior arrived.

This law guardian of ceremonies and sacrifices did not change who the Israelites were: children of their heavenly Father. This law guardian could not take away the inheritance that was theirs through the promise of the coming Savior given to Adam and Eve and Abraham. And now that the Savior had come, the relationship to the chaperone changed. The Galatians could declare, "We've never had it so good." You and I too can now say, "We've never had it so good." Paul invites everyone to look at the evidence that this is true. He lays out a list of the blessings we have.

There is the obvious truth of what we are.

²⁶**In fact, you are all sons of God through faith in Christ Jesus.**

Sometimes the Bible calls us children of God. Here the Bible calls all of us, male or female, "sons of God." In biblical language that reflects the culture of that time, the word *son* has the legal connotation of inheritance. A son is different from a slave or servant. A son has standing in his father's house. He stands to inherit all that belongs to his father. What does Jesus say to his believers in that scene of the final judgment? "Come, you who are blessed by my Father, *inherit* the kingdom prepared for you" (Matthew 25:34, emphasis added).

Also, there is another comfort to knowing that we are all sons of God through faith in Christ Jesus. This word links each of us with God's only begotten Son.

Remember that scene on the banks of the Jordan River when Jesus was baptized, the heavens opened, the Holy Spirit descended as a dove, and the Father spoke? "This is my Son, whom I love. I am well pleased with him" (Matthew 3:17). If Jesus is our Substitute—as the Bible teaches—and if God is pleased with Jesus—as the Father says—then God is well pleased with you and me too, not because of us but because of his Son's perfection in our place. We've never had it so good!

In fact, what the Father said to Jesus at his baptism he says to you and me at our baptism: "This is my son, this is my daughter, whom I love. I am well pleased with him, with her."

²⁷**Indeed, as many of you as were baptized into Christ have been clothed with Christ.**

The Bible paints a lot of pictures to portray what God does for us in Baptism. Here in Galatians, Paul links our sonship with God to our baptism. In Baptism, God writes our name into his family register. Paul says here that we are "clothed with Christ" through Baptism, that we have put on Christ, that we are wrapped in the robes of Christ's righteousness. What Christ earned for us he wraps around us.

Jesus once told a parable about a man who tried to crash a wedding reception without a wedding garment (Matthew 22:1-14). He was thrown out on his rear into the outer darkness. In ancient times, wedding garments were provided by the host of the royal banquet. To not wear it, to come stomping in with your barn boots or track shoes, would be an insult to the host. I may come to God "just as I am" but only with the plea that his blood was shed for me (CW 814).

Listen to Isaiah: "He has clothed me in garments of salvation. With a robe of righteousness he covered me" (Isaiah 61:10). What does Jeremiah call the coming Savior? "The LORD Our Righteousness!" (Jeremiah 23:6). Here in Galatians Paul says, "As many of you as were baptized into Christ have been *clothed with Christ.*" Remember the glorified believers on the pages of Revelation? "They have washed their robes and made them white in the blood of the Lamb" (Revelation 7:14). Remember the traditional Communion prayer? "Take off from [the communicants] the spotted garment of the flesh and of their own righteousness, and adorn them with the righteousness purchased with Thy blood." Or the old hymn? "Jesus, your blood and righteousness my beauty are, my glorious dress" (CW 573). We've never had it so good!

To these early Galatian Christians, enticed by the Judaizers to imagine that the Gentiles were at best distant relatives to Jesus, Paul tells them that they are all one family in Christ Jesus.

²⁸**There is not Jew or Greek, slave or free, male or female, for you are all one and the same in Christ Jesus. ²⁹And if you belong to Christ, then you are Abraham's descendants and heirs according to the promise.**

There are a lot of distinctions among people on this side of heaven—some man-made, some God-ordained. God himself has crafted distinctions between men and women, husbands and wives, parents and children, and government and citizens.

But when it comes to our standing with God, the distinctions melt away. Princes and peasants, preachers and parishioners, bosses and workers, Jews and Gentiles, male and female—all come to God on the same level playing field: as sinners fully redeemed by Christ, sons and heirs of God through faith, and one in Christ Jesus. All Christians can claim to be Abraham's spiritual offspring and heirs of all that belongs to Christ. We've never had it so good.

"Let's talk about this 'heir' business again," says Paul.

⁴:¹**What I am saying is this: As long as the heir is a young child, he is no different from a slave. Although he is owner of everything, ²he is still under guardians and managers until the day set by his father. ³So also, when we were younger children, we were enslaved under the basic principles of the world. ⁴But when the set time had fully come, God sent his Son to be born of a woman, so that he would be born under the law, ⁵in order to redeem those under the law, so that we would be adopted as sons.**

Going back to this picture of the Law of Moses as a guardian or chaperone, the *paidagogos* from the Greek culture of that day, Paul says, "Listen, as long as the heir is a child, he is no different from a household slave, even though he is the legal heir of the whole estate. He is still under guardians and managers until he comes of age."

The son of a wealthy business tycoon will one day inherit the whole business from his father, but the son is not allowed to boss around his father's employees when he is only six years old. He is subject to his father's discipline and the rules of the house like any other child until he comes of age.

Paul says that's the way it was when we were spiritual children, living under the elementary principles of the world as well as the ABCs of the Law of Moses. The people of Israel were tightly controlled in their worship, their diet, and even what they could touch without becoming ceremonially unclean. A parent may pick up an item in a store to examine it and yet forbid the child to touch anything on the shelves. That's how it was with the Israelites until Christ finally came.

"When the set time had fully come, God sent his Son to be born of a woman, so that he would be born under the law, in order to redeem those under the law, so that we would be adopted as sons."

Entering this world from outside of it, existing before it, the Son of God, the second person of the Trinity, set foot on our planet as true God yet born of the virgin Mary. He came to redeem those under the law by keeping the law for us, to ransom us when we were held hostage by sin, death, and the dark powers. All this God did that we might be adopted as sons and live forever as members of the Father's household. We've never had it so good!

One of the great privileges that goes with being a son and heir is that "God sent the Spirit of his Son into our hearts to shout, '*Abba*, Father!' "

⁶Because you are sons, God sent the Spirit of his Son into our hearts to shout, "*Abba*, Father!" ⁷So you are

no longer a slave, but a son. And if you are a son, then you are also an heir of God through Christ.

Think here of Luther's explanation to the opening words of the Lord's Prayer: "Our Father in heaven."

With these words God tenderly invites us to believe that he is our true Father and that we are his true children, so that we may pray to him as boldly and confidently as dear children ask their dear father. (Martin Luther, *Luther's Catechism*, Northwestern Publishing House, 2017, p. 243)

In a beautifully trinitarian way of talking, Paul says that God the Father sends God the Holy Spirit from God the Son into our hearts. And the Holy Spirit inhabits our hearts, folds our hands, and talks into the ear of God for us saying, "*Abba*," the Aramaic word for "father."

Paul says also in Romans 8:26 that "the Spirit himself intercedes for us with groans that are not expressed in words." When we are too tired, too weak, too confused, too sad, or too overwhelmed, the Holy Spirit lends us a hand, translates our prayers into the ear of God for us, and intercedes for us. He edits, corrects, refines, and perfects our prayers to match what God wants, which is always what is best for us.

Sometimes our parents were quite right when they said, "You've never had it so good!" But our heavenly Father is *always* right. The prodigal son came to see this in the pigsty of that far country. He never had it better than when he was in his father's house (Luke 15:11-32).

Perhaps more instructive for many of us is the older brother who never ran away in the first place. He fails to see how blessed he has been all along. He says, "Look, these many years I've been serving you . . ." That's how he sees things. This is why he is so joyless, so miserable. He has forgotten how good he's got it!

Listen to how the father talks to his oldest son: "Son, did you forget that? You are my son, not my slave." Sadly it had never occurred to the son to wake up each morning and say something like "Father, today I am especially happy to be your child." The father continues, "Son, you are always with me, and all that I have is yours. My son, my heir, did you forget that? No wonder you are so sad. No wonder you are so angry. No wonder you have a hard time being happy for this brother of yours who came home again."

Now, my baptized friends, you sons and heirs, robed in the righteousness of your Friend who died for you and invites you to the banquet of his gospel, there is *nothing* in any far country that is better than *anything* you already have here in your Father's house all the time in all the years to come. We've never had it so good.

Lines From Luther

But to put on Christ according to the Gospel is a matter, not of imitation but of a new birth and a new creation, namely, that I put on Christ Himself, that is, His innocence, righteousness, wisdom, power, salvation, life, and Spirit. (*Luther's Works*, Vol. 26, p. 352)

He does not say: "Through Baptism you have received a token by which you have been enlisted in the number of the Christians;" this is what the sectarians imagine when they make of Baptism merely a token, that is, a small and empty sign. But he says: "As many of you as have been baptized have put on Christ." That is: "You have been snatched beyond the Law into a new birth that took place in Baptism. Therefore you are no longer under the Law, but you have been dressed in a new garment, that is, in the righteousness of Christ." Therefore Paul teaches that Baptism is not a sign but the garment of Christ, in fact, that Christ Himself is our garment. Hence Baptism is a very powerful and effective thing. (*Luther's Works*, Vol. 26, p. 353)

It is impossible ever to decide what God wills and what is pleasing to Him, except in His Word. This Word makes us certain that God cast away all His wrath and hatred toward us when He gave His only Son for our sins. The sacraments, the power of the keys, etc., also make us certain; for if God did not love us, He would never have given us these. Thus we are overwhelmed with endless evidence of the favor of God toward us. (*Luther's Works*, Vol. 26, p. 388)

GALATIANS

4:8-20
Enslaved by False Gods or Set Free by the True God?

Let us briefly review the backstory behind this God-breathed letter to the Galatians. On Paul's first missionary journey, he established several congregations in ancient Asia Minor. These churches included those in southern Galatia that had both Jewish and gentile converts to Christ. On the way home from this first journey, Paul retraced his steps, reinforced the gospel message in these infant congregations, and saw to it that pastors were put in place. On his second missionary journey, he visited these congregations in Galatia again. Then he moved on to Macedonia and Greece.

Paul has just settled into his ministry in the Greek city of Corinth when he gets word: Troublemakers, the Judaizers, have infiltrated the Galatian churches. These are Jews who had converted to Christianity but maintained that faith in Christ is not enough. They assert that Gentiles also need to be circumcised and keep the laws of Moses. They undermine the Bible's clear teaching that believers, whether Jew or Gentile, are saved by grace alone through faith alone in Jesus Christ alone.

Paul is astonished that the Galatians have deserted the gospel so quickly. With an intensity born of white-hot love, Paul sets before the Galatians only two ways to live out their lives: enslaved by false gods or set free by the true God.

> **⁸Formerly, when you did not know God, you were slaves to those who by nature are not gods. ⁹But now that you know God, or rather are known by God, why are you turning back again to the basic principles that are weak and miserable? Do you want to be enslaved by them all over again? ¹⁰You carefully observe days, months, seasons, and years. ¹¹I am fearful about you, that somehow my labor for you was wasted.**

Paul aims his astonishment at the gentile believers here, those who grew up in the idol-worshiping Greek world. Have you forgotten, he asks, the way things used to be, when you did not know the true, triune God? "You were slaves to those who by nature are not gods." You lived your lives on the merit system. You figured that whatever gods there were could be bought off with money or noble works. But you would never know if the works you were doing were the right works, if the money was enough money. You dreaded death each day. Everyone around you was dying. You knew you must die too. Then what? It was all a bitter bondage, wasn't it? You were enslaved by gods that, as it turns out, were not gods at all.

But then you came to know the true, triune God. Better still, you came to be known by him . . . for he knew you before you came to be . . . he recognized your face amid the millions upon millions for whom he was dying on the cross. He knew you personally before you knew him. He called you by name. It was not your decision but his choice to love you, redeem you, and adopt you in the gospel waters of Baptism. He called you by this gospel to believe in him. You were set free by this gracious God. You stopped wondering if you were good enough. You weren't. You stopped worrying whether you could do enough. You couldn't. You came to trust in him who was more than good enough for you, who did more than enough in your place. The chains so tightly squeezing your conscience fell clattering to the floor. You were set free to live and to be unafraid to die. You moved from the slavery of the merit system to the freedom of the grace system.

"So now," writes Paul to his beloved Galatians, "why are you turning back again to the basic principles that are weak and miserable? Do you want to be enslaved by them all over again? You are entertaining doomed, dangerous ideas. You are falling victim to another gospel that is no gospel at all. You are letting these false teachers take you back to the dark ABCs of the merit system, to slavery and fear.

"You observe the days, months, seasons, and years of the ceremonial law—Sabbath days, new moon celebrations, Old Testament festivals—not out of Christian liberty, not as teaching tools—as using a church year calendar may remind you of Christ's work of redemption—but out of a slavish obedience to these observances that were a shadow of the Christ to come. Even the Old Testament believers knew that the law could only show them their need for Christ and that they could be saved only by looking in faith to the coming Savior."

The odd thing here is that Paul is addressing a church likely composed of more gentile than Jewish believers. These recent converts had been set free from their slavery to the merit system of false gods, but now they are reverting back to the merit system while wearing the label of Christ! If you are going to follow the merit system, then it makes no difference if you do this in the name of Allah or Christ, whether you are called heathen or Christian. It is godless idolatry all the same, no matter how saintly and pious it may appear. Forsaking grace and running back to a meritorious works system is like trying to strengthen yourself with weakness, to enrich yourself with poverty, to cure heart disease by getting cancer. Paul wonders out loud if he has labored among the Galatians in vain.

"Listen," writes Paul in a softer tone, "do you really want to be enslaved by false gods or set free by the true God?"

> [12]**I beg you, brothers, become like me, for I also became like you. You did me no harm.** [13]**You know that, because of a weakness of the flesh, I preached the gospel to you the first time.** [14]**And you did not despise or disdain the test my flesh gave you. Instead, you welcomed me as an angel of God, as Christ Jesus.** [15]**So where is this blessed attitude of yours now? Yes, I can say for a fact that, if it were possible, you would have plucked out your eyes and given them to me.** [16]**So then, have I become your enemy by telling you the truth?**

Paul takes on a fatherly tone with his Galatian brothers and sisters. He entreats them, appeals to them, "I take no pleasure in scolding you. But I am bound to warn you that the religious pills being fed to you are not candy; they are poison. The spiritual spot you are being pointed to is not a playground; it is a killing field. Ask yourselves who really loves you: the preachers who tell you a different gospel they want you to hear or the faithful pastors who tell you what you need to hear? May you imitate the prodigal son, who finally figured out that life in the far country, out from under the eye of his father, was no freedom at all, but slavery."

"Think back," writes Paul, "to how gladly you received me and the gospel message that I brought to you on that first missionary journey. I came to you under less than ideal circumstances because of a weakness of the flesh, a bodily ailment."

Some think Paul may have had malaria that he picked up in the lowlands around Perga. To recover, he sought the higher elevation of Galatia, and that is how the Galatians came to hear the gospel. Others think he may have had some disfiguring eye disease that made it difficult to even look at Paul when he preached. There is his remark here that, if possible, the Galatians would have gouged out their own eyes and given them to him. And there is his remark in the final chapter of Galatians that he writes with large letters. Was this the so-called thorn in the flesh that Paul mentions in 2 Corinthians 12:7-10? Or is this business about plucking out their eyes just an expression as when people talk about giving others the shirts off their backs? Whatever it was, Paul's troublesome, unglamorous condition did not turn the Galatians off. They did not scorn him or his message. They welcomed him as an angel of God, as though Christ himself walked among them. This gospel was their heart-pounding joy at no longer being enslaved by false gods but set free by the true God.

Do you notice how intensely personal Paul is here? No one hears the gospel in a vacuum. The glad tidings of Christ's living, doing, dying, and rising are wrapped in fond memories of those who brought them to us. We recall a kind Sunday school teacher who took a liking to us, a Christian teacher who was patient, a Christian friend or pastor who was there when the roof caved in, Christian parents who took the time to read a Bible lesson and pray with us when they tucked us in at night and took us to worship services even when we fussed about going—so that the house of God became our oasis in the desert that daily living can bring. These were the people who cared, who corrected and comforted us. "Now after all this," asks Paul, "have I become your enemy by telling you the truth?"

"These Judaizers are not your friends," writes Paul.

> [17]Those people are eager to win you over, but not in a good way. Rather, they want to alienate you, so that you will be eager for them. [18]But it is always a good thing to have someone eager in a good way—not just when I am present with you.

Paul's words might remind us of a book that some of us used to read to our children when they were little: *Never Talk to Strangers.* These false prophets who are taking you back to the salvation-by-merit system, to the slavery of false gods, make much of you, writes Paul. They flatter you, telling you how wonderful you are. Both false and true prophets are eager to win people over but for far different reasons. The Judaizers want to shut out the Galatians from Paul and win people over to a bogus gospel. A parent aims for the love and affection of a child but not for the same reasons as an outsider intent on doing damage to the family.

Paul's love for the Galatians is pure, even tender. He tries to call them back from the dangerous detour they are taking.

> [19]My children, I am suffering birth pains for you again until Christ is formed in you. [20]I wish I were present with you now and could change my tone, because I am perplexed about you.

Here Paul talks in terms any mother can understand—the labor pains that precede the bringing of life into the world. Paul does not wish to form the Galatians in his image. He wants them to be formed in the image of Christ, that Christ be formed in them. Writing to the Galatians from a distance is a painful process for Paul. He wishes he could be there in person, to see the look in their eyes, to have them see the love in his eyes, to hear the tone of their reaction so that he can adjust the tone of his voice in kind. Paul is perplexed about them. How will they turn out? Who will they take after? Will they be enslaved again by false gods or set free by the true God?

The desired answer is as simple as the name into which we were adopted in Baptism: "In the name of the Father and of the Son and of the Holy Spirit." In those gospel waters, the Father who created us, the Son who redeemed us, and the Spirit who sanctifies us set us free—free from sin's guilt and slavery, free to serve with glad hearts the One who loves us with an everlasting love.

These words, once spoken with splashes of water on our heads, are spoken over our heads at the start of each service. Each time God wants us to hear the chains snap and fall, clattering to the floor. Listen: "In the name of the Father and of the Son and of the Holy Spirit."

Lines From Luther

> Here someone may say: "If the Galatians sinned in observing days and seasons, why is it not sinful for you to do the same?" I reply: We observe the Lord's Day, Christmas, Easter, and similar holidays in a way that is completely free. We do not burden consciences with these observances; nor do we teach, as did the false apostles and as do the papists, that they are necessary for justification or that we can make satisfaction for our sins through them. But their purpose is that everything be done in the church in an orderly way and without confusion, so that external harmony may not be disturbed; for in the spirit we have another kind of harmony. . . . Most of all, however, we observe such holidays to preserve the ministry of the Word, so that the people

may gather on certain days and at certain seasons to hear the Word, to learn to know God, to have Communion, to pray together for every need, and to thank God for His spiritual and temporal blessings. And I believe that this was the chief reason why the fathers instituted the Lord's Day, Easter, Pentecost, etc. (*Luther's Works*, Vol. 26, pp. 411,412)

He [Paul] also teaches by his example that pastors and bishops should take a fatherly and motherly attitude, not toward the ravenous wolves (Matt. 7:15) but toward the miserable, misled, and erring sheep, patiently bearing their weakness and fall and handling them with the utmost gentleness. Nor can they be called back to the right way by any other means, for a more severe rebuke is more likely to anger them than to bring them back to their senses. (*Luther's Works*, Vol. 26, p. 413)

Thus we today are forced to hear from the Sacramentarians [who rejected the real presence of Christ's body and blood in the Lord's Supper] that by our stubbornness we are splitting the love and harmony of the churches, because we reject their doctrine of the Lord's Supper. It would be more appropriate, they say, if we shut our eyes just a little, especially since the only danger involved here is that because of this one doctrine we may arouse such discord and controversy in the church; for, after all, they do not disagree with us on any article of Christian doctrine except the one doctrine of the Lord's Supper. To this I reply: "A curse upon any love and harmony whose preservation would make it necessary to jeopardize the Word of God!" (*Luther's Works*, Vol. 26, pp. 424,425)

GALATIANS

4:21-31
A Tale of Two Cities

Have you seen the bumper stickers with the coexist symbol? The bumper stickers spell out the word *coexist* using symbols from various religions including Islam, Buddhism, Judaism, Wicca, and Christianity—all in an effort to promote religious tolerance.

If this implies that persecuting people for their religion is unacceptable, who of us would disagree? If this means that as Christians we will want to be kind, patient, and respectful as we try to lead souls trapped in error to the truth of the gospel, we would say, "Of course." Without much thought, maybe some Christians think that this is all the coexist bumper stickers mean.

But the postmodern mind-set in our pluralistic society of many religions is preaching a different message with these coexist symbols. The gospel of postmodernism says that all religions and all lifestyle choices—straight, gay, lesbian, transgender, or whatever—are equally valid; that one person's truth is as good as another person's truth; that there is, in fact, no such thing as absolute truth; and that if there is a heaven, all roads and all religions lead there.

No Christian worthy of the name can salute the idea that all religions and lifestyles are equally true or valid without betraying him who said, "I am the Way and the Truth and the Life. No one comes to the Father, except through me" (John 14:6). Paul has been making this very point in this letter to the Galatian Christians.

Paul's point is that the false gospel of the Judaizers and the true gospel of Christ cannot coexist as equally correct. He has said this in plain words. Now he uses an illustration from Bible history. It starts with a tale of two mothers, a tale of two sons, and finally, with a nod to the novel by Charles Dickens, *a tale of two cities*. Let's look at the biblical historical event itself, what it illustrates, and what it means for you and me.

Let us review the event itself first.

> **²¹Tell me, you who want to be under the law, are you really listening to the law? ²²For it is written that Abraham had two sons, one by the slave woman, and one by the free woman. ²³However, the son by the slave woman was born according to the flesh, but the son by the free woman was born through a promise.**

Some of the recent converts in the Galatian congregations are blindly following the poisonous teachings of the Judaizers. They want to wear the Christian label and yet live under the Mosaic covenant law and be saved by personal obedience to the law. "Tell me," says Paul, "you who want to be under the code of laws given through Moses, don't you listen to what Moses himself wrote in the book of Genesis? For it is written that Abraham had two sons, one by the slave woman, and one by the free woman. However, the son by the slave woman was born according to the flesh, but the son by the free woman was born through a promise."

Do you remember the historical event Paul is talking about? God promised Abraham a son through whom the Savior would come. But Abraham was getting old. His wife, Sarah, was barren. The flame of faith began to flicker in the breeze of divine delays and disappointments. Abraham believed God's promise that a son would come from his own aging body, a son through whom the Christ would one day descend. Sarah believed too.

But by now they have been waiting for ten years. They are ten years older. Perhaps Sarah reasons, "Yes, Abraham, a son from your own body but probably not from mine. Things are not happening here. Neither one of us is getting any younger. And after all, God helps those who help themselves, doesn't he?"

Figuring God needs a little push, Sarah takes the bull by the horns—arranging surrogate motherhood. She gives her maidservant, Hagar, to Abraham to produce a legal heir. The custom of the day not only allowed a childless wife to give her household servant to her husband but in some cases also demanded it. Archeologists digging around in ancient Nuzi, in what is now Iraq, have uncovered marriage contracts in which a bride promised to give her husband a servant if she herself could have no children. So Hagar, Sarah's servant, gives birth to Ishmael (Genesis chapter 16).

Abraham and Sarah doubtless mean well. But it's plainly a case of using human devices to achieve God's purpose and ultimately interfering with God's plan. It is weak faith that rushes ahead of God with means and methods not pleasing to him. God makes this plain.

Eventually, however, after all the long years, the sound of laughter can be heard coming from Sarah's tent—Isaac (the name means "laughter"), the promised son, was born (Genesis chapter 21). She who once laughed in doubt and skepticism now laughs for joy. She had the son whose miraculous birth in her old age has been viewed as a foreshadowing of a far more miraculous birth centuries later by a virgin undefiled in Bethlehem.

But soon there is tension in the tents of Abraham. The time comes when little Isaac is weaned from his mother's breast. In that culture the child may be three or four years old. Abraham throws a big celebration at this rite of passage. Hagar and Ishmael are in attendance, of course. By this time, Ishmael may be 17 or 18 years old—a strapping young man. He takes to mocking the little child Isaac.

The Hebrew word for "mocking" has the same root as Isaac's name. Was Ishmael making a joke out of Isaac's name—calling the little boy laughable—and calling the promise that Isaac would be the heir of all that God had promised Abraham laughable too? We sense it is more than sibling rivalry, more than an older brother teasing a younger brother. Paul makes this point in Galatians 4:29 when he says, "The one who was born according to the flesh [Ishmael] persecuted the one who was born according to the Spirit [Isaac]." This bullying was a repeated pattern in the divided household.

Sarah knows that this is an intolerable situation. There must be a parting of ways. It is surely grief to Abraham also, for Ishmael too is his son. But the Lord himself lifts any burden of concern from Abraham, telling him that this is all part of the divine plan. It is through Isaac that the people of promise and eventually the Savior will come. Ishmael too will become the father of a great nation, but the promises of God must take precedence over fleshly ties. So off into the desert Hagar and Ishmael are sent.

So this tale of two cities involves two mothers and two sons—one born of a slave woman and one born of a free woman; one born in the usual way according to the flesh but the other born as a result of God's promise. This also illustrates two covenants, says Paul.

²⁴These things can be used as an illustration; namely, the women are two covenants. One is from Mount Sinai, bearing children into slavery. This is Hagar. ²⁵You see, this Hagar is Mount Sinai in Arabia, and she corresponds to present-day Jerusalem, because Jerusalem is in slavery along with her children. ²⁶But the Jerusalem that is above is free. She is our mother. ²⁷For it is written:

Rejoice, barren woman who does not give birth. Break forth and shout for joy, woman who does not suffer birth pains, because the barren woman has more children than does the woman who has a husband.

The illustration is simply this: Hagar and her son, Ishmael, exemplify Mount Sinai, which was counted as part of Arabia in ancient times. Hagar, the slave woman, and her slave son represent Sinai where the law would be given to Moses, a law that holds us in bondage. Paul says that all of this is also in line with the present Jerusalem—for the inhabitants of the physical city in Paul's day were living in bondage still. Even though Christ himself walked in their streets, the majority of them rejected his free salvation in favor of continuing to live under the law. So Hagar, Ishmael, Sinai, and the physical city of Jerusalem—all illustrate living out one's life in the wrong city and covenant; in a state of slavery to the law, unable to keep it and so unable to be saved by it.

But Paul says that there is another line of spiritual descent illustrated by the history of Abraham's life. Sarah, the free woman, and her son, Isaac, born as a result of a gracious promise, are tied to the Jerusalem above—not just to heaven as such but also to the spiritual Jerusalem that looks to heaven rather than to earth for salvation, the believers who look to Christ's doing, dying, and rising rather than to any human's doing, paying, and working.

Just as Sarah was barren and thought incapable of having a child, so the holy Christian Church—the Jerusalem born from above—is despised in the world as a little flock and thought to be barren. The law-oriented mega churches are large precisely because the sinful nature is drawn to this city and covenant of bondage. But by the preaching of the gospel, the despised church in which the Word is purely proclaimed and the sacraments rightly administered becomes our mother, who has given birth to countless children who are the free sons and daughters of the King through faith in him.

Now, writes Paul, this is what all this means for you and me.

28Now you, brothers, like Isaac, are children of the promise. 29But just as back then the one who was born according to the flesh persecuted the one who was born according to the Spirit, so this is also the case now. 30But what does the Scripture say? "Throw out the slave woman and her son, because the son of the slave woman will certainly not receive the inheritance with the son of the free woman." 31For this same reason, brothers, we are not children of a slave woman, but of the free woman.

The long and short of this tale of two cities is that there are not—and cannot be—two ways of being saved: one by human merit and one by faith in the promised Savior. The true heirs of Abraham are those who believe in Christ alone for their salvation. Any other way is a false way, a way of slavery, bondage, and condemnation. Now, as then, the person born in the ordinary way persecutes the one born by the power of the Spirit. Now, as then, the two cannot harmoniously coexist regarding their radically different religious assumptions or share in the same inheritance.

What this means for us is that by faith in Christ we are not children of the slave woman but of the free woman. Jesus said, "If you remain in my word, you are really my disciples. You will also know the truth, and the truth will set you free" (John 8:31,32). The Jews bristled at Jesus' words. They believed they were already free simply by being physical descendants of Abraham. Jesus made the same point as Paul: "Amen, Amen, I tell you: Everyone who keeps committing sin is a slave to sin" (John 8:34).

What a great light dawns on the heart of any of us when we are set free from a relationship that is based on fear, punching the clock, logging the hours, hating the boss, keeping up appearances, and itching to get out of the relationship! We are set free to enter a relationship that is based on pardon, on confidence that we are loved—and so glad to serve, eager to please, wanting to be where our Lord is, wanting to do what he wants, loving what he loves, and loving him.

Living in this city and covenant is so different, so liberating. Instead of thinking "I *have* to go to church," it is "I *want* to go to church to hear God's Word and enjoy fellowship with my brothers and sisters in Christ." Instead of "I *have* to obey my parents," it is "I *want* to please the parents God gave me." Instead of "My spouse is such a ball and chain," it is "My spouse is the chief opportunity God has given me to show the same unselfish, sacrificial love that Christ has shown to me." Instead of "What can I get away with?" it is "How can I joyfully live today as a baptized child of my Father on the way to heaven?" Now in which city shall we live?

Lines From Luther

> Therefore Sarah, or Jerusalem, our free mother, is the church, the bride of Christ who gives birth to all. She goes on giving birth to children without interruption

until the end of the world, as long as she exercises the ministry of the Word, that is, as long as she preaches and propagates the Gospel; for this is what it means for her to give birth. (*Luther's Works*, Vol. 26, p. 441)

Therefore anyone who teaches or urges either the Law of God or human traditions as something necessary for righteousness in the sight of God does nothing other than give birth to slaves. And yet such theologians are regarded as the best; they earn the applause of the world and are the most prolific mothers, that is, have an infinite number of disciples. (*Luther's Works*, Vol. 26, p. 443)

"But I have not done anything good and am not doing anything now!" Here you neither can nor must do anything. Merely listen to this joyful message, which the Spirit is bringing to you through the prophet: "Rejoice, O barren one that dost not bear!" It is as though He were saying: "Why are you so sorrowful when you have no reason to be sorrowful?" "But I am barren and desolate." "Regardless of how much you are that way, since you have no righteousness on the basis of Law, Christ is still your Righteousness. He became a curse for you; He has redeemed you from the curse of the Law (Gal. 3:13). If you believe in Him, the Law is dead for you. As much as Christ is greater than the Law, that much better is the righteousness you have than the righteousness of the Law. Moreover, you are not barren either, because you have more children than she who has a husband." (*Luther's Works*, Vol. 26, pp. 447,448)

GALATIANS

5:1-12
The Emancipation Proclamation

He told folks it was coming. On January 1, 1863, in the midst of our nation's Civil War, President Abraham Lincoln issued an executive order proclaiming that any slaves in the ten states then in rebellion against the Union were and would be "thenceforward, and forever free."

We know this executive order as the Emancipation Proclamation. The timing was strategic. It galvanized the Union war effort. The results were not immediate. Only about 50 thousand of the more than 3 million slaves affected by the proclamation were immediately set free. Most slaves awaited the gradual advancement of the Union armies before the Emancipation Proclamation made a difference to them personally. In fact, it wasn't until June 19, 1865, two months after Lincoln's assassination, that the Union army, under Major General Gordon Granger, arrived in the remotest confederate state of Texas to enforce the executive order. To mark the occasion, in 2021 the United States established a new holiday called Juneteenth.

Lincoln understood all the difficulties and complexities even as he issued the proclamation. In the end, Lincoln became known as "the Great Emancipator."

To *emancipate* means to "set free." These chapters of Paul's letter to the Christians in Galatia tell us that the ultimate Great Emancipator is Jesus Christ. His doing, dying, and rising for all is the beating heart of the gospel, the good news, the ultimate emancipation proclamation. Paul bids us to stand firm *in* it and stand guard *over* it.

5:1It is for freedom that Christ has set us free. Stand firm, then, and do not allow anyone to put the yoke of slavery on you again.

How do you picture freedom? Maybe you think of the freedoms enshrined in our constitution's Bill of Rights—freedom of religion, freedom of speech, freedom of the press, freedom to assemble, and so on. Maybe you think of the emancipated lives we live every day in our own country compared to the tightly monitored and controlled lives of people in China, Iran, or Saudi Arabia. Or maybe you remember that freedom isn't free, that it has come at the high price of someone else's blood and sacrifice, at the expense of soldiers lying face down in the mud in places such as Gettysburg and Normandy.

The freedom in which Paul bids the Galatians and us to stand firm is infinitely deeper and more enduring. Joseph was confined to Pharaoh's dungeon, but no ghosts of guilt could hold his conscience captive (Genesis chapter 39). The dying thief next to our Lord was fastened to a cross with nails, but no condemnation of the law could bar him from the pardon and paradise given him by Christ (Luke 23:39-43). Peter lay chained in prison between armed guards, but no stone walls could rob the sleeping apostle of the peace that passes understanding (Acts 12:1-11).

Our own separate shackles of past misdeeds, debt, disease, or dull routine cannot deprive us of this deeper and more enduring freedom.

"It is for freedom that Christ has set us free," says Paul. He who was handcuffed in the garden and bound for trial before the chief priests and Pilate, who was tied to the whipping post and crowned with thorns, who was fastened to a cross and locked in a cold tomb, has risen from the grave's dark prison. Luther's Easter hymn explains our emancipation, "Christ Jesus lay in death's strong bands for our offenses given; but now at God's right hand he stands and brings us life from heaven" (CW 439:1/440:1). When Christ died and rose, he sent forth his apostles with an emancipation proclamation: the good news that we were "thenceforward, and forever free."

As when Lincoln issued his proclamation, there are those who have not yet heard it. There are those who, even after hearing it, do not believe it. There are those who, even after hearing it and believing it, fail to enjoy it fully or even forfeit their freedom by going back to their old masters.

The Judaizers have been undermining Paul's gospel of freedom in the Galatian congregations. They are adding small print at the bottom of the page of the emancipation proclamation of free forgiveness through faith in Christ. Their doctored message insists that faith in Christ is not enough, that a right standing with God depends on keeping the ceremonial laws of Moses that pointed ahead to Christ and became obsolete when Christ came. Representing all this was the covenant of circumcision. "It is for freedom that Christ has set us free," says Paul. Christ has not set us free to submit again to the yoke of slavery, to the bondage of trying to earn our way.

"It is too easy to go back to the old masters," says Paul. "You need to stand firm in this gospel freedom. The alternative is unthinkable."

> **²Look, I, Paul, tell you that if you allow yourselves to be circumcised, Christ will be of no benefit to you. ³I testify again to every man who allows himself to be circumcised that he is obligated to do the whole law. ⁴You who are trying to be declared righteous by the law are completely separated from Christ. You have fallen from grace.**

It isn't the rite of circumcision itself that Paul attacks here, for as he himself says in the lines following, "In Christ Jesus neither circumcision nor uncircumcision matters." Early on, Paul had his young associate Timothy circumcised to remove barriers to their mission work among the Jews. But on another occasion he flatly refused to have his coworker Titus circumcised because the Judaizers demanded it as something necessary for salvation and not as a matter of liberty. It is in this sense that Paul says, "Look, I, Paul, say to you that if you accept circumcision, that is, as a work that merits favor with God, Christ will be of no benefit to you." In other words, what's the point of Christmas, Good Friday, and Easter if they're not enough? If you still have to pay your way? And how will you ever know whether you have done or paid enough?

Those who rely on the law for salvation are rightly called "martyrs of the devil," according to Luther. Such people live miserable lives here, sweating and straining to work off sin's guilt and power, and they will live miserable lives hereafter because they have turned down the emancipation Christ won for them. It is a wicked thing to make Christ useless, to call him a liar when he tells us he has paid for our sins.

"If you want to play this game," says Paul, "then you must remember that the person who relies on circumcision is now obligated to keep the whole covenant law of Moses, the entire code of laws given to the Israelites at Mount Sinai." No cafeteria religion here: picking what you want—circumcision or the Sabbath Day—but leaving the rest—laws of ceremonial purification or dietary regulations about kosher foods. It's all or nothing. Either Christ has fulfilled the law entirely, or he has left us to do it. But you can't have it both ways.

Paul is blunt: "You who are trying to be declared righteous by the law are completely separated from Christ. You have fallen from grace." Either the law or Christ has to yield. Either we spend our lives listening to the jail keeper of the law who tells us we are never going to get out of this prison of our past sins, this dungeon of never doing enough—or we tune in to the voice of our great emancipator who says, "A bent reed I will not break; a dimly burning wick I will not snuff out. . . . Take heart, your sins are forgiven. . . . I will remember them no more. . . . Come to me, all you who are weary and burdened, and I will give you rest" (Isaiah 42:3; Matthew 9:2; Jeremiah 31:34; Matthew 11:28).

Now stand firm in this freedom that through the Holy Spirit we have by faith as we eagerly wait for the hope of righteousness.

⁵Indeed, through the Spirit, we by faith are eagerly waiting for the sure hope of righteousness.

The "hope" of righteousness? Don't we already have it by faith in Christ? Of course. But we are not yet as conscious of this right standing with God as we are of our sin. "Faith is being sure about what we hope for, being convinced about things we do not see" (Hebrews 11:1). What we are painfully aware of, what we are terribly conscious of, are our sins and failures, the cemetery that waits, and God's wrath and judgment. What we struggle to hang on to by faith is the freedom we have in Christ, the righteousness he has wrapped around us. We often do not feel forgiven or see it. So we must follow not the voice of our conscience but the Word of God. In a sure hope, we wisely embrace the concluding words of that comprehensive hymn on grace, "By Grace I'm Saved": "I cling to what my Savior taught and trust it, whether felt or not" (ELH 226:10).

⁶For in Christ Jesus neither circumcision nor uncircumcision matters. Rather, it is faith working through love that matters.

The only thing that matters is faith in the One who has set us free from sin and guilt, from death and damnation. "This faith works or expresses itself through love," says Paul. We are not saved *by* our love. Love is simply the language of faith. We are saved by faith alone, but saving faith is never alone. As a pear tree produces pears, as an apple tree bears apples, and as water is wet, so faith produces works of love. Real faith is not a dead-head knowledge that simply parrots certain facts—that Noah built an ark, that Jesus was born in Bethlehem and died on a cross. Faith is a Spirit-wrought, childlike trust that Jesus did all these things for *me* and for *you*. This very real faith is not a couch potato. It is always looking for ways to love those at our side and those who have not yet heard this emancipation proclamation. Mary of Bethany expressed her faith and love with the precious perfume she poured on the feet of Christ (John 12:1-8). The good Samaritan's faith worked through love when he scuttled his whole day to take care of the man mugged on the road (Luke 10:25-37). The faith of Nicodemus and Joseph of Arimathea sprang to action when they removed Jesus' lifeless body from the cross and gave their Lord a decent burial (John 19:38-42).

"It is in this freedom of forgiveness that we need to stand firm and over which we need to stand guard," says Paul.

> **⁷You were running well! Who cut in on you, so that you are no longer persuaded by the truth? ⁸This persuasion is not from the one who calls you. ⁹A little yeast works through the whole batch. ¹⁰I am confident in the Lord that you will have no other opinion than this. But the one who is trying to disturb you will pay the penalty, whoever he is. ¹¹Brothers, if I am still preaching circumcision, why am I still being persecuted? Then the offense of the cross has been abolished. ¹²If only those who are upsetting you would also cut themselves off!**

Once saved, always saved is not a biblical teaching. Judas lost his faith. So have others. Paul is worked up about the damage the Judaizers had done to the souls in Galatia. "You were running well!" he says to his flock. "Who cut in on you, disrupted your stride, tripped you up? This persuasion is not from the one who calls you. This counterfeit gospel of meritorious works is not something you learned from Christ."

"A little yeast works through the whole batch," says Paul. A pinch of yeast permeates the whole lump of dough. Deny Christ in one point and you risk denying him entirely. Every false teaching eventually grows, spreads, expands, and takes aim at the beating heart of the gospel: our pardon in Christ.

"I am confident," says Paul, "that you will not drink this poison. Those who are causing this trouble will bear the penalty. They will answer to the Good Shepherd whose sheep they have led astray. Their persecution of what I am preaching is evidence of the truth." And with a remark made under inspiration of the Holy Spirit, Paul says something that shocks the people who never expect their preacher to offend. He says, "If only those who are upsetting you would also cut themselves off!" He utters a harsh wish on these false teachers, saying that if they remain that insistent on circumcision, he hopes the knife slips, that these mutilators of souls would mutilate themselves.

Long before our great emancipator stepped into our world at Bethlehem, his voice was heard on the pages of Isaiah: "The Spirit of the LORD God is upon me, because the LORD has anointed me to preach good news to the afflicted. He sent me to bind up the brokenhearted, to proclaim freedom for the captives" (Isaiah 61:1). He told us this emancipation proclamation was coming. Now we have heard it. Let us believe it, stand firm *in* it, and stand guard *over* it. For if the Son sets us free, we shall be free indeed!

Lines From Luther

This is the freedom with which Christ has set us free, not from some human slavery or tyrannical authority but from the eternal wrath of God. Where? In the conscience. For Christ has set us free, not for a political freedom or a freedom of the flesh but for a theological or spiritual freedom, that is, to make our conscience free and joyful, unafraid of the wrath to come (Matt. 3:7). This is the most genuine freedom; it is immeasurable. When the other kinds of freedom— political freedom and the freedom of the flesh—are compared with the greatness and the glory of this kind of freedom, they hardly amount to one little drop. For who can express what a great gift it is for someone to be able to declare for certain that God neither is nor ever will be wrathful but will forever be a gracious and merciful Father for the sake of Christ? (*Luther's Works,* Vol. 27, p. 4)

Let us remember this well in our personal temptations when the devil accuses and terrifies our conscience to bring it to the point of despair. He is the father of lies (John 8:44) and the enemy of Christian freedom. At every moment, therefore, he troubles us with false terrors, so that when this freedom has been lost, the conscience is in continual fear and feels guilt and anxiety. When that "great dragon, the ancient serpent, the devil, the deceiver of the whole world, who accuses our brethren day and night before God" (Rev. 12:9-10)—when, I say, he comes to you and accuses you not only of failing to do anything good but of transgressing against the Law of God, then you must say: "You are troubling me with the memory of past sins; in addition, you are telling me that I have not done anything good. This does not concern me. For if I either trusted in my performance of good works or lost my trust because I failed to perform them, in either case Christ would be of no avail to me." (*Luther's Works*, Vol. 27, p. 11)

Therefore if Christ appears in the guise of a wrathful judge or lawgiver who demands an accounting of how we have spent our lives, we should know for certain that this is not really Christ but the devil. (*Luther's Works*, Vol. 27, p. 11)

GALATIANS

5:13-26

Liberty or License?

We are edging toward the end of Paul's epistle to the Galatians. The smoke of battle and the clatter of weaponry have been rising from the page. The battle was joined when the Judaizers infiltrated Paul's Galatian congregations as the devil's double agents. Like many others throughout history, and in our own day also, they did not deny that people should believe that Jesus died for our sins and rose again. But they maintained that faith in Christ was not enough. Instead of proclaiming salvation by faith in Christ alone, they said that salvation came by faith *and* works.

In this Magna Carta of Christian liberty, Paul drives a wooden stake through the heart of this false teaching. With eternity at stake, Paul throws down the gauntlet of the uncompromising and unconditional gospel of Christ. We are saved by grace alone through faith alone in Christ alone. We cannot thrive without knowing this. The stricken conscience can find no comfort without believing this.

There is no truth of God that Satan does not twist. So it is with the gospel of God's free grace in Christ. Is the grace of God a liberty *from* sin or a license *to* sin? Liberty or license? You and I might think the answer is obvious. But in every time and place, in every Christian congregation, in every human heart as it is by nature, there is the inclination to "turn the grace of our God into a license for sin" (Jude 4). That's why Paul spends the closing chapters of this letter teaching us that we have been set at liberty to live *for* Christ.

Our liberty sets us free to love, says Paul.

> [13]**After all, brothers, you were called to freedom. Only do not use your freedom as a starting point for your sinful flesh. Rather, serve one another through love. [14]In fact, the whole law is summed up in this one statement: "Love your neighbor as yourself." [15]But if you keep on biting and devouring one another, watch out that you are not consumed by one another.**

Paul says, "After all, brothers, you were called to freedom. Only do not use your freedom as a starting point [literally, a base of operation, a launchpad] for your sinful flesh."

There is a liberty that is really no liberty at all but, rather, a foul bondage. Eve became the first *liberated* woman—declaring her independence from God only to hide in the bushes bound by shame, guilt, and fear. The prodigal son wanted to be free, out from under the influence of his father. Instead, he ended up fettered with his own failure in a pigsty of a far country (Luke 15:13-16). The rich fool wanted to be free of financial worry. So he staked his life on bigger and fuller barns, a grand retirement fund. But he had to leave it for the relatives to fight over in probate court. On that very night the jail keeper of death slammed the door on his life (Luke 12:13-21). For all these people, their so-called liberty was a lie—a lonely, bitter bondage.

None of this is the fault of the gospel. People do not live godless lives because they believe in the free forgiveness of Christ. They live godless lives because they do not truly trust in Christ in the first place. Anyone who truly knows what it is to have the debt of a lifetime canceled by Christ, to have all the IOUs torn up, gets a new and grateful heart that loves Christ, wants what God wants, thinks the way God thinks.

Now we are set free to serve one another through love, says Paul. If you think about it, every one of the Ten Commandments is a way of showing love—love for God and love for one another. "In fact, the whole law is summed up in this one statement: 'Love your neighbor as yourself.'"

So the liberty we have in the wounds of Christ produces a love that gladly fulfills the law, not a permissive attitude that breaks it, a disregard for others that bites and devours them like a pack of snarling dogs, or a twisted liberty that says, "My neighbor is not worthy of my love. He has this fault and that fault. She offended me years ago. They got in my face last week."

Of course, Jesus could say that about us. He could have said it two thousand years ago. He could have said, "These people are not worth loving, not deserving enough that I should die for them." As with Christ, so with Christ's people: Love is as love does. Love is not merely a feeling, an emotion, an idea that we wish people well in some abstract way. Love comforts the afflicted, puts up with a neighbor's annoying rudeness, is patient with a cranky spouse, and shows respect to a parent.

This is what real liberty is: to be set free from bondage to our sinful selves and to be at liberty to live by the spirit rather than by the flesh, in accordance with our Christian nature rather than in agreement with our old Adam, that is, our sinful nature.

The Holy Spirit has created within every believer a spirit or new nature that opposes the flesh or sinful nature we were born with. Paul now has more to say about this.

> [16]What I am saying is this: Walk by the spirit, and you will not carry out what the sinful flesh desires. [17]For the sinful flesh desires what is contrary to the spirit, and the spirit what is contrary to the sinful flesh. In fact, these two continually oppose one another, so that you do not continue to do these things you want to do. [18]But if you are led by the spirit, you are not under the control of the law.

All Christians experience this internal and ongoing civil war. What Paul describes here is the constant state of war going on in the hearts of believers, in your heart and mine. Luther was fond of describing a Christian as *simul justus et peccator*—at one and the same time a saint and a sinner.

Have you noticed how the Bible portrays the heroes of faith? They are not plaster saints. They are people like you and me. They have fears, suspicions, scruples, anger, and joy like other people. Elijah takes on an evil army on the summit of Mount Carmel, calling down fire from heaven. Then when Jezebel puts out a contract on his life, he runs into the desert, plops himself down under a tree, and whines from his discouraged heart that he wants to die. But he does not give up on God entirely. He pours out the complaints of his sad heart to God, listens to what God tells him, and then goes back to work (1 Kings chapters 18,19). Peter calls to Jesus in the storm, "Lord, if it is you, command me to come to you on the water." But halfway there, the big fisherman sees the waves looming larger than his Lord, and he begins to sink. But he does not totally give up the struggle. He cries out, "Lord, save me!" (Matthew 14:22-33). Peter, James, and John all enter Gethsemane intent on remaining loyal in the most critical hour of the Savior's life. But weary from grief and tension, they drop off to sleep. Jesus sizes it up: "The spirit is willing, but the flesh is weak" (Matthew 26:36-41).

My spiritual nature—my new nature—listens to a sermon, reads a text from the Bible, and sings a familiar hymn. A bright light shines down on my path. The clouds lift. I can almost touch the face of God. I feel enlightened, empowered, equipped to handle anything the devil, the world, and my own flesh may throw at me. A great peace descends.

But then something happens, maybe only 15 minutes later. A nagging problem returns to snap at my heels. Disappointment rolls in like a morning fog over a valley. An accident, an illness, the loss of a loved one, or sheer fatigue knocks me off my feet. I have a bad day at school or at work. The kids push all the buttons. A fight breaks out in the car on the way home from church. And guess what? Every Bible passage I ever learned, every sweet hymn verse that ever moved me suddenly flies right out of my head. I can't remember a single thing the preacher said. It's all gone.

I have to go back to the Word again, back to the hymns again, back to the sermons again, to recharge, regroup—at liberty to live by the spirit, no longer driven by the law. With my Christian nature in the driver's seat of my life and my sinful nature in the backseat—better yet, in the trunk or better still, tied to the back bumper by a long rope—I enjoy freedom. Ah, liberty!

You don't have to have a PhD to figure out the difference between liberty *from* sin and license *to* sin. The works of the flesh, of the sinful nature, are obvious, says Paul.

¹⁹Now the works of the sinful flesh are obvious: sexual immorality, impurity, complete lack of restraint, ²⁰idolatry, sorcery, hatred, discord, jealousy, outbursts

of anger, selfish ambition, dissensions, heresies,
[21]envy, murders, drunkenness, orgies, and things
similar to these. I warn you, just as I also warned you
before, that those who continue to do such things will
not inherit the kingdom of God.

Paul lists sexual relations outside of marriage and moral
impurity of every kind, including trashing one's marriage vows,
homosexual behavior, and pornography. He mentions idolatry
that honors any god other than the triune God; sorcery that
probes the dark powers; hatred, strife, and jealousy that scream
life is all about us; fits of anger and rivalries that turn homes into
battlegrounds where husbands, wives, and children cringe; dissensions, divisions, heresies, and envy that poison the fellowship
of believers; and drunkenness, binge drinking, and wild behavior that bring shame to the name of Jesus.

Paul's list is random. You can add any number of other
mutations of wickedness that, unless followed by repentance,
forfeit the kingdom of heaven—murder of one's unborn child
in a clinic or with a pill, utter contempt for Christ's Word and
sacraments. When these things are all cloaked beneath excuses
such as "God wants me to be happy . . . Jesus will forgive me
anyway . . . Times have changed," then the liberty *from* sin is
twisted into a license *to* sin. Those who live like this, not just in
a moment of weakness (as any child of God may stumble and
daily repent) but who "continue to do such things" as habitual
behavior, who keep living like this, and who make this their
unrepentant lifestyle—they "will not inherit the kingdom of
God." If you willfully and persistently live in sin, you drive out
faith. You won't go to heaven. Period.

But don't miss the grace note in that word *inherit*. That little
word *inherit* says that you and I are the adopted sons and daughters of the King. An inheritance is a gift. It is not something

earned. It is earned by the life and labors of someone else. In order for us to get it, someone has to die. Christ earned it. Christ died. Now everything that belongs to Christ belongs to us. His perfect life is ours. His payment for sin on the cross is our payment in full. His resurrection is our affirmation of life everlasting. This is the inheritance we stand to lose if we imagine that we can turn our liberty *from* sin into a license *to* sin.

Infinitely better than this highway to hell is the liberty we have in Christ to bear fruit.

> **²²The fruit of the spirit is love, joy, peace, patience, kindness, goodness, faithfulness, ²³gentleness, and self-control. Against such things there is no law. ²⁴Those who belong to Christ Jesus have crucified the sinful flesh with its passions and desires. ²⁵If we live by the spirit, let us also walk in step with it. ²⁶Let us not become conceited, provoking one another and envying one another.**

Did you catch the contrast? "The *works* of the sinful flesh" as opposed to "the *fruit* of the spirit." All these things Paul now lists are various grapes on the same cluster. Jesus said, "I am the Vine; you are the branches. The one who remains in me and I in him is the one who bears much fruit, because without me you can do nothing" (John 15:5). We have been set free to bear the fruit of love, joy, and peace in our relationship with God; to bear the fruit of patience, kindness, and goodness to those God has placed at our side and in our path; and to bear the fruit of faithfulness, gentleness, and self-control as we carry out our duties as parents, pastors, teachers, farmers, merchants, or manufacturers.

We are a new people, a free people, brought to life by the Spirit and so keeping in step with the Spirit, rather than running the way of the sinful flesh. Insofar as we keep in step with this Christian nature, we are no longer conceited or full of ourselves, picking fights and envying the gifts and callings of others around us. All those chains fall clattering to the floor, for we have been set free. We have crucified, disabled, and put to death the sinful nature with its passions and desires. We are set free to say with the poet, "What pleases God, that pleases me" (CW 799).

Paul wrote something like this elsewhere: "All of us who were baptized into Christ Jesus were baptized into his death" (Romans 6:3). Commenting on this, Dr. Siegbert Becker used to talk about how, as children in a Lutheran elementary school, he and his schoolmates would go to the church and sing the same hymn for every funeral—"Jerusalem, Thou City Fair and High" (CW 1993, 212). Then they would follow the pallbearers as they carried the coffin out to the cemetery right next to the church. Before the committal service, they would lower the casket into a pine box vault in the grave. One man would go down and nail the cover to the box. Then the committal service would begin as an elder of the church stood with his foot on a shovel stuck into the mound of dirt. When the pastor got to the words "Earth to earth," the elder threw the first shovelful of dirt into the grave. It hit the pine cover with a loud thud. "Earth to earth." Boom! "Ashes to ashes." Boom! "Dust to dust." Boom! It was heartrending. Tears flowed. It brought the reality home. Years later, when Dr. Becker became a pastor himself, this is what he thought of every time he baptized a child: "I baptize thee in the name of the *Father* [Boom!] and of the *Son* [Boom!] and of the *Holy Ghost* [Boom!]." Every baptism is a funeral for our old sinful nature. We died to sin. We were set at liberty to live for God. Liberty or license? Which would we rather have? Remember: Every inappropriate license has an expiration date. Christ is coming. The party will end. But liberty? Liberty is forever!

Lines From Luther

It is unavoidable that you are offended frequently and that you offend in turn. You see much in me that offends you; and I, in turn, see much in you that I do not like. If one does not yield to the other through love on matters like this, there will be no end to the argument, discord, rivalry, and hostility. Therefore Paul wants us to walk by the Spirit, so that we do not gratify the desires of the flesh. It is as though he were saying: "Even though you are aroused to anger or envy against an offending brother or against someone who does something unkind to you, still resist and repress these feelings through the Spirit. Bear with his weakness, and love him in accordance with the command: 'You shall love your neighbor as yourself.' For your brother does not stop being your neighbor simply because he lapses or because he offends you, but that is the very time when he needs your love for him the most." (*Luther's Works*, Vol. 27, p. 66)

I remember that Staupitz used to say: "More than a thousand times I have vowed to God that I would improve, but I have never performed what I have vowed. Hereafter I shall not make such vows, because I know perfectly well that I shall not live up to them. Unless God is gracious and merciful to me for the sake of Christ, and grants me a blessed final hour when the time comes for me to depart this miserable life, I shall not be able to stand before Him with all my vows and good works." (*Luther's Works*, Vol. 27, p. 73)

GALATIANS

6:1-10
Blessed or Bitter Harvest?

Let's jump into the middle of the pond here. Paul writes in verse 7 of this chapter, "Whatever a man sows, he will also reap." You and I might say, "You get out of it what you put into it."

Surely the great theme of Paul's letter to the Galatians, the beating heart of the gospel, is that we are saved not by our works but through faith in Christ alone. But Paul also points out that faith in Christ is never alone. It always bears fruit. Jesus himself said so, "I am the Vine; you are the branches. The one who remains in me and I in him is the one who bears much fruit, because without me you can do nothing" (John 15:5). The Lord's brother, James, says it in another way in his New Testament letter: "Faith without works is dead" (James 2:26). Loving God's word, living the Christian life, laying our requests before God in prayer—these all are the vital signs, the heartbeat and respiration of a real and living faith.

Now "whatever a man sows, he will also reap." The faith of an Abraham, the courage of a King David, the doctrinal clarity of a Paul—such things do not grow in the parched desert sands of doing your own thing, neglecting Word and sacrament, or loving things and using people. This poses a question for all of us: Will there be a blessed or bitter harvest?

A blessed or bitter harvest may be related to how we deal with the souls around us.

> ⁶:¹**Brothers, if a person is caught in some trespass, you who are spiritual should restore such a person in a spirit of humility, carefully watching yourself so that you are not also tempted.**

As a good pastor, Paul draws a distinction between stubborn and unrepentant souls whose professed faith is a sham, who commit themselves to a sinful life of the flesh—who certainly will not inherit the kingdom of heaven unless they repent— versus the brother or sister who is, as Paul puts it, "caught in some trespass."

The Greek word for "caught" has in it the idea of being taken by surprise. As Luther puts it in his explanation to the Fifth Petition of the Lord's Prayer—"Forgive us our sins"—"We daily sin much." Paul himself describes the relentless inner battle every Christian endures between the sinful nature and the new Christian nature (Romans 7:14-25). So the Bible paints the great heroes of faith with warts and all—Noah having too much wine in an unguarded moment, Abraham passing his wife off as his sister to save his own hide from danger, Moses losing his patience with the people of Israel, David having too much time on his hands and a wandering eye, Elijah losing heart, and Peter running scared under pressure. The list is endless. Your name and mine are on that list too.

Sometimes one person is weak and the other is strong. Sometimes the roles are reversed. We get caught by surprise.

We surprise ourselves. We could just kick ourselves. We know better. But what if a brother or sister gets tangled up in some sin? Or doesn't even see it as a sin right away? Or starts going down a dangerous path?

It is not love to ignore it. A sin of weakness can easily morph into an impenitent lifestyle. The harvest could be eternally bitter. Real love reaches out, says something. "But," says Paul, "you who are spiritual"—not any better than the person you are talking to, knowing how often you have fallen on your own face, aware of your own weakness, having tasted the forgiving Word of God yourself—"you who are spiritual should restore such a person in a spirit of humility." This word for "restore" is the same word the gospels use when telling us that the disciples were "mending" their nets. Our motive and demeanor in reaching out to someone caught up in some sin are not to be self-righteous, better-than-thou, or condescending but gentle to try to fix what is broken, mend a heart that is torn, or put back in order what is out of line.

"Pay attention to your approach," says Paul, "carefully watching yourself so that you are not also tempted." In a movie about men trapped in the Alaskan wilderness called *The Edge*, the brilliant Charles Morris, played by Anthony Hopkins, utters a famous encouragement. He says, "What one man can do, another can do." It becomes the group's mantra of survival in the savage wilderness. "What one man can do, another can do."

But long before Charles Morris uttered that word of encouragement, the church father Augustine uttered this word of warning, as quoted by Luther: "There is no sin that one man has committed that another man could not commit" (*Luther's Works*, Vol. 27, p. 112). Read that again: "There is no sin that one man has committed that another man could not commit."

We see on the news men and women in orange jumpsuits and handcuffs standing in front of a judge, or we hear of horrendous crimes that leave us shaking our heads in disgust. We wonder how anyone could fall so hard, so far, so fast. We are quite certain this could never happen to us.

But then we remember David on the balcony or Peter in the courtyard. Or we remember how close we came to doing something. And the old saying just has to cross our minds: "There, but for the grace of God, go I." Or that word from Psalm 130:3, "If you, LORD, kept a record of guilt, O Lord, who could stand?" "There is no sin that one man has committed that another man could not commit."

"So guard your own heart," says the apostle, "carefully watching yourself so that you are not also tempted."

The path to a blessed harvest consists of humbly bearing one another's burdens.

> **²Bear one another's burdens, and in this way fulfill the law of Christ.**

In bearing one another's burdens, we fulfill the law of Christ. We follow his model, his pattern, his example. Bearing our burdens is what Christ did.

The prophet Isaiah described Jesus this way: "Surely he was taking up our weaknesses, and he was carrying our sufferings." And again, "We all have gone astray like sheep. Each of us has turned to his own way, but the LORD has charged all our guilt to him" (Isaiah 53:4,6).

When you and I try to comfort someone who is in misery, we sometimes say, "I know what you're feeling," or "I know what you're going through." If we have endured a very similar adversity in our lives, we may indeed have a good idea of what that person is enduring. Still, each person's pain and pleasure are unique to that individual. Try as we may to sympathize and empathize, as rightly as we may follow the Bible's encouragement to "rejoice with those who are rejoicing; weep with those who are weeping" (Romans 12:15), we can never fully enter into other people's pain. Whether a headache or a heartache, we can go only up to the door of their infirmities and sorrows. We can perhaps peek inside the house of their heart a bit, but we cannot take their place. We cannot suffer the side effects of their chemo and radiation treatments for them. We cannot gasp for air for them as their lungs fill up with fluid. We cannot take on the sting of their private guilt. We cannot pick up their tab or take their punishment at the judgment seat of the Most High. This only Jesus could do. This only Jesus has done. The infirmities he took up were ours. The sorrows he carried were ours. The sins for which he suffered were ours. By his life and in his death, he fully entered into our pain, picked it up, made it his own, and carried it away.

In Article IV of the Smalcald Articles in the Lutheran Confessions, Luther talks about the different ways in which the gospel gives us counsel and help. "First," he says, "through the spoken Word. . . . Secondly, through Baptism. Thirdly, through the holy Sacrament of the Altar. Fourthly, through the power of the keys." But then Luther adds this neat little phrase: "And also through the mutual conversation and consolation of brethren."

"The mutual conversation and consolation of brethren" is what happens when Christians take the gospel out the church door each week and talk about it around the dinner table, shine its light on a lost soul, share its comfort with a sad friend, explain its teachings to a confused mind, or sound its warning to a loved one going down a dangerous detour. "The mutual conversation and consolation of brethren" happens at pastor and teacher conferences, at church fellowship hours, and out in the garage while working on a car. It is quite often unscheduled, unpredictable, and unscripted.

Such conversation and consolation are rooted in the Scriptures; in the Bible history lessons we read to our children; in church services, Bible classes, Sunday school and Christian classrooms; in a parent's heart-to-heart talk with a child about the one thing needful (Luke 10:42 King James Version); in a grandparent's hand of encouragement on a grandchild's shoulder; and in a hundred other ways. Paul points us to the source of this conversation and consolation when he says, "Indeed, whatever was written in the past was written for our instruction, so that, through patient endurance and the encouragement of the Scriptures, we would have hope" (Romans 15:4). He also says, "I myself am convinced about you, my brothers, that you yourselves are also full of goodness, filled with complete knowledge, and able to instruct one another" (Romans 15:14).

It is a Christlike thing to help someone bear a burden, to lighten a load, to bind up a broken heart with words the Good Shepherd has loaned us, to help that abused fellow traveler on the road, to apply the ointment of the gospel to a bruised and embarrassed heart.

On the other hand, it produces a bitter harvest if we approach one another with arrogance.

> **³For if someone thinks he is something when he is nothing, he deceives himself. ⁴Let each person test his own work, and then he will take pride in regard to himself and not his neighbor. ⁵For each man will bear his own burden.**

"If someone thinks he is something when he is nothing, he deceives himself." It is a dangerous thing to be a legend in one's own mind. Remember our Lord's story of the Pharisee and the tax collector (Luke 18:9-14). The Pharisee evaluates himself by a downward glance at the crooked tax collector. He does not confess his sins. He compares his sins. So he comes off smelling like a rose.

The tax collector or publican, on the other hand, sees himself as God sees him and confesses, "God, be merciful to me, a sinner!" (Luke 18:13).

Jesus says of the tax collector, "I tell you, this man went home justified rather than the other, because everyone who exalts himself will be humbled, but the one who humbles himself will be exalted" (Luke 18:14). This is basic: "Nothing in my hand I bring, simply to thy cross I cling" (CW 839:3).

Now, says Paul, ensure a blessed rather than a bitter harvest by supporting this preaching and teaching ministry of the free gospel.

> **⁶Let the one who is taught the word share all good things with his teacher.**

The word Paul uses for "taught" and "teacher" is the one from which we get the word *catechism*. It refers to the oral preaching and teaching of the Word. Paul told the Corinthians, "Those who preach the gospel are to receive their living from the gospel" (1 Corinthians 9:14). Jesus said, "The worker deserves his support" (Matthew 10:10). Certainly, the showbiz-for-Jesus hucksters who shake down widows and orphans to support their lavish lifestyles are a scandal to the church and a disgrace to the gospel. But as Luther liked to remark, so is a church that once filled the bellies of ten fat monks in support of false teachings and now refuses to support one honest preacher of the gospel. Luther saw it as a barometer of what people really value.

Here is the principle behind what Paul is saying:

> **⁷Do not be deceived. God is not mocked. To be sure, whatever a man sows, he will also reap. ⁸Indeed,**

the one who sows for his own sinful flesh will reap destruction from the sinful flesh. But the one who sows for the spirit will reap eternal life from the spirit. ⁹Let us not become weary of doing good, because at the appointed time we will reap, if we do not give up. ¹⁰So then, as we have opportunity, let us do good to all people, and especially to those who belong to the household of faith.

All farmers understand the risk they must take in order to reap. It is an axiomatic principle that Paul sets down elsewhere: "The one who sows sparingly will also reap sparingly. The one who sows generously will also reap generously" (2 Corinthians 9:6). Who expects acres and acres of corn when he or she plants only one handful of seed? Of course there is a risk! Seed costs money. It is a large investment. And then farmers do an odd thing with this investment. They throw it in the dirt and leave it. "Of course," we might say, "that's what you're supposed to do with seed. It will grow." Precisely! But there are no guarantees.

However good the seed may be, however good the ground may be, the seed is at the mercy of the elements. Drought may wither it. Too much sun may scorch it. Too much rain may rot it. Hail and driving winds may destroy it. Insects may devour it.

But what farmer refuses to run the risk, refuses to plant? Who buys one bucket of seed and then hopes for the best? Not for a moment do the farmers think of the seed as wasted, even though when they go to bed at night, all that expensive seed lies out there in the dirt under the moonlight, ready to sprout and grow in ways they cannot fully understand or control.

So it is with our entire Christian life, says Paul. We invest in so many other areas of life—sowing the seeds of education, entertainment, and athletics. Worse, we may be tempted to sow the wild oats of sinful pleasures. But God will not be mocked.

We cannot turn up our nose at the Almighty and get away with it. If we sow to the sinful flesh, we will reap corruption and destruction. If we sow for the spirit, for the new nature, we will reap what God has promised—life eternal.

Only let us not become weary of doing good, weary perhaps because we do not see immediate results. At the appointed time we will reap. The people around us, all of them—especially those of the household of faith—are opportunities awaiting our love until the blessed harvest. "Those who wait for the LORD will receive new strength. They will lift up their wings and soar like eagles. They will run and not become weary. They will walk and not become tired" (Isaiah 40:31).

Lines From Luther

In the doctrines of the faith nothing should seem small or insignificant to us, as though we should or could surrender it. For the forgiveness of sins pertains to those who are weak in faith and morals, who acknowledge their sin and seek forgiveness, but not to the subverters of doctrine, who do not acknowledge their error and sin but defend them vigorously as though they were truth and righteousness. (*Luther's Works*, Vol. 27, pp. 108,109)

If you see some brother in terror because of a sin of which he has been guilty, run to him, and extend your hand to him in his fallen state. Comfort him with sweet words and embrace him with your motherly arms. The obdurate and stubborn, who fearlessly and smugly persist and continue in their sins, you should rebuke sharply. But those who are overtaken in a trespass and sorrow and grieve over their fall should be encouraged and instructed by you who are spiritual. And this should be done in a spirit of gentleness, not of zeal for righteousness or cruelty. (*Luther's Works*, Vol. 27, p. 111)

Love is sweet, kind, and patient—not in receiving but in performing; for it is obliged to overlook many things and to bear with them. In the church faithful pastors see many errors and sins which they are obliged to bear. In the state the obedience of subjects never lives up to the laws of the magistrate; therefore if he does not know how to conceal things, the magistrate will not be fit to rule the commonwealth. In the family many things happen that displease the householder. But if we are able to bear and overlook our own faults and sins, which we commit in such great numbers every day, let us bear those of others as well, in accordance with the statements: "Bear one another's burdens" and "You shall love your neighbor as yourself" (Lev. 19:18). (*Luther's Works*, Vol. 27, pp. 113,114)

GALATIANS

6:11-18
Cross Brand

Some years ago the Hershey Company teamed up with Starbucks to help each other sell chocolate and coffee. NAPA Auto Parts promoted NASCAR with its advertising and vice versa. Coca-Cola was the official brand of the Olympics to benefit both entities. The NBA aimed to make $100 million by adding advertising patches to its uniforms. This sort of thing is called cross marketing or cross branding. Each product is branded by the other's label. They are identified with each other.

Pardon the play on words, but the Bible talks about some "cross branding." There is a cross that marks the life of Christ, the cross to which he was nailed, the cross by which he redeemed us from sin, death, and the dark powers. As the doorposts of the Israelites in Egypt were marked with blood from an unblemished lamb (Exodus chapter 12) so that death might pass over their homes and lives, so we by faith are branded with the blood of Christ crucified. What does a pastor say at a baptism? "Receive the sign of the cross on the head and heart. . . ." Jesus brands us as his own, identifies himself with us before the Father's throne with the cross that marked his life.

There is a cross that marks our lives too. It is not a cross by which we redeem ourselves. Christ has already done that. That's his brand on us. But there is a cross of suffering for the sake of Christ that automatically marks us as his when we come to faith. As Christ gladly bore the cross of suffering to save us, so we who bear his brand now gladly bear the cross of suffering for him to confess his name, serve him, and identify ourselves as his own.

So the Bible talks about Christ's cross and our cross. Here in the last lines of Paul's fiery letter to the Galatians, he talks about this cross brand. There are questions each of us must answer about the cross: Am I ashamed of it? Am I proud of it? Am I marked by it?

[11]See what large letters I am writing to you with my own hand.

Paul launches into these last lines of his letter with a personal touch, a little window into his personal habits as an inspired writer. Like other writers of his day, Paul often dictated his letters to a scribe, a sort of recording secretary. Amid the final verses of Paul's letter to the Romans, his secretary even butts in to say, "I, Tertius, who wrote down this letter, greet you in the Lord" (Romans 16:22).

You and I crumple up pieces of writing paper and throw them away with little thought. But in Paul's day, writing materials such as parchment, papyrus, or vellum were fairly scarce and pricey. The mechanics of writing were somewhat of a specialized skill. It wasn't as though people could just erase something or hit the delete button. Scribes or secretaries were skilled in writing neat, orderly, and small letters. Some could write as neatly as any word processor. They knew how to get the most out of a sheet of expensive parchment.

But the very fact that letters were often dictated to a scribe could create problems—forgeries and false claims. In Paul's second letter to the Thessalonians, he urges the Christians there to not get distressed by what he calls "a letter thought to be from us" (2 Thessalonians 2:2). He then closes his letter with an assurance, "This greeting is written by me, Paul, with my own hand. This is a distinguishing sign of how I write in every letter" (2 Thessalonians 3:17). He ends his letter to the Colossians by saying, "This greeting is written by me, Paul, with my own hand" (Colossians 4:18).

Now in these final paragraphs of Paul's letter to the Galatians, he writes, "See what large letters I am writing to you with my own hand." Did Paul, out of his sheer agitation over the false teachers who were troubling the Galatians, write this entire letter without the help of a scribe? Luther thought so. Or were only these final paragraphs in his own handwriting? Why in "*large* letters"? Was it that, despite the expense of writing materials, he wanted to show them his love and concern? Is it here that we have further evidence of Paul's eye trouble, that the brilliant and inspired apostle had to write in large letters like a small child? Had his hands been crippled by the cruel tortures he had endured for Christ? All of these are fascinating questions that the Bible does not answer. But Paul's point is clear. "See what large letters I am writing to you with my own hand," he says, like a school teacher wrapping on a desk to get the students' attention.

Attention, class! Are you ashamed to be branded with the cross of Christ crucified, to be identified with him who died such a shameful death for you? These Judaizers who have been schmoozing you certainly are.

¹²Those who want to look good in the flesh are the ones who are trying to compel you to be circumcised. Their only reason is so that they are not persecuted

> **for the cross of Christ. ¹³As a matter of fact, those who are circumcised do not keep the law themselves. But they want to have you circumcised, so that they can boast about your flesh.**

What's the deal with these Judaizers? Three things, says Paul: They want to look good, they want to avoid persecution, and they don't practice what they preach.

Wanting to force Gentiles to be circumcised and adhere to the Mosaic covenant ceremonies, the Judaizers would be pleasing to non-Christian Jews. Also, they could sidestep the painful persecution from the Jews that Paul and others had endured for preaching the free grace of God in Christ. Alongside this, Paul says, "These teachers who want you to toe the line don't do it themselves. They play cafeteria with the law of God, picking and choosing what they wish to do but bragging that they have gotten you Galatians to jump through their hoops."

In short, they are ashamed of the cross brand. Paul said to the Corinthians, "The message of the cross is foolishness to those who are perishing" (1 Corinthians 1:18). Think about this. We wear shiny gold crosses on our lapels and as jewelry around our necks. We put crosses on our steeples and our altars.

But what if you came to church some Sunday morning, bowed your head for prayer, looked up at the altar, and there, unmistakably, where the cross used to be, you saw a replica of an electric chair? How would you react? Or what if your daughter came downstairs in the morning wearing a gold hangman's noose around her neck? Creepy.

Well, the people of the Roman Empire in Paul's day saw a cross as something far more creepy. The cross was used for the most depraved criminals, for slaves and non-Romans, as a terror tactic to keep order in the far-flung provinces. It was illegal to crucify a Roman citizen. Now think of what Paul's sermon could be in some city of the empire: "I have come to tell you about the Savior, the Son of God himself, who came down from heaven to save us." The Romans might say, "This Savior must be a great general or warrior." That's how the Romans saved people. But then Paul says, "Do you know how this Savior saved us? He saved us by dying on a cross!" You can imagine how Christians themselves might be tempted to feel ashamed to tell others about a Savior who was crucified.

But you may say, "We don't have that problem with crosses anymore." True enough. But there are other things about the gospel we may be tempted to walk away from, to pretend we don't see because we are too embarrassed. How embarrassed are we that the Bible teaches a six-day creation or that little babies are born sinful and need the gospel as offered in Baptism? Do we fear the condescending smirks of those who mock the virgin birth, the miracles of Christ, the resurrection of Christ, or the word-for-word inspiration of the Bible? Are we intimidated by people who get their religious beliefs from television, the *National Enquirer*, or fictional novels such as *The Da Vinci Code*? How easy has it ever been to tell people that there is only one way to heaven—by grace through faith in Jesus Christ? How ashamed are many churches to wear the brand of the cross, who substitute entertainment or pop psychology for the everlasting gospel?

For Paul, the question about the cross brand is "Am I proud of it?" Here's his answer.

> **14Far be it from me to boast, except in the cross of our Lord Jesus Christ, through which the world has been crucified to me and I to the world. 15In fact, in Christ Jesus circumcision or uncircumcision does not matter. What matters is being a new creation. 16Peace and mercy on those who follow this rule, namely, on the Israel of God.**

Elsewhere Paul says, "I am not ashamed of the gospel" (Romans 1:16). That's another way of saying, "I'm proud of the gospel." Here is Paul's famous line: "Far be it from me to boast, except in the cross of our Lord Jesus Christ." Similarly, we sing the hymn "In the Cross of Christ I Glory" (CW 529). To boast, to glory in the cross of Christ, is the opposite of boasting about all the glamorous things we are doing. It is the opposite of bragging that we are basically good. It is to boast that we have no other hope but Christ Jesus.

All the world's ideas about salvation, all its desires and proud ambitions, have been crucified to us, are dead to us. "They no longer hold any attraction for me," says Paul. Moreover, we are crucified to the world. As long as we are branded by the cross of him who loved us, the world regards us as crucified, strung up in shame, dead and gone, yesterday's news.

So what? If football fans are proud to wear their favorite team's jerseys even if they live in an opposing team's area, if baseball fans wear their team's hats even in cities where opposing teams are based, then why should we be ashamed to wear the cross brand in an often hostile world? For a Christian, confessing Christ boldly is as natural to the new spirit as water being wet, fire being hot, and grass being green. "I believed; therefore, I have spoken," said the psalmist—words repeated by Paul in the New Testament (Psalm 116:10; 2 Corinthians 4:13). Despite resistance from the sinful nature, our love of Christ's cross may still show itself in daily life.

When the dying thief on the cross next to Jesus came to faith in the 11th hour of his life, what was the first thing he did? He confessed Christ to the other thief, rebuking him for his unbelief and trying to lead him to repentance. When the leaders of the Lutheran Reformation presented the Augsburg Confession to His Imperial Majesty Charles V in 1530, they placed on the title page of that great confession the words of Psalm 119:46: "I will speak of your testimonies before kings, and I will not be put to shame."

God forbid that we should boast in anything in heaven above or on earth beneath—anything except the cross of our Lord Jesus Christ by which we have been made new creations who love what Christ loves and think the way Christ thinks. This is the cross that makes us the real Israel of God by faith in Jesus, whether we are Jews or Gentiles. As Paul said earlier in this letter to the Galatians, "Understand, then, that those who believe are the children of Abraham" (Galatians 3:7).

When we are proud of his cross, we will surely be marked, branded by, and identified by the cross he bids us bear.

[17]**Finally, let no one cause me any trouble, because I bear the marks of the Lord Jesus on my body.** [18]**The grace of our Lord Jesus Christ be with your spirit, brothers. Amen.**

The word Paul uses here for "marks" was also used for the brand of ownership on animals. Paul had all kinds of marks on his body for the sake of Jesus. He cataloged the beatings and abuse he suffered for the sake of Christ (2 Corinthians 11:23-33). Here he closes out his letter, knowing that the Judaizers, the false teachers, are listening in. He says, "Take it or leave it, believe it or reject it. I have no intention of compromising it or dressing it up. Grace is what it is, the beating heart of the gospel. You can just let me be, for I bear on my body the marks of Jesus—the whippings, the stonings, the imprisonments. Take it or leave it."

For all who belong to Jesus, there will be a cross. No cross, no Christian. We need not seek one or lay one on someone else.

God will give each Christian the cross he or she must bear for Christ along with the strength to bear it. There is a cross brand. We are his. He is ours.

Paul writes one last line before sending his letter, "The grace of our Lord Jesus Christ be with your spirit, brothers." As Ezekiel rushed about to mark the foreheads of God's elect (Ezekiel chapter 9), as the blood of the lamb marked the lives of the Israelites in Egypt (Exodus chapter 12), so we are marked with the blood of our Savior. This is the grace of God that will never lead us where his love shall not keep us. To that we say with Paul a hearty "Amen!"

Lines From Luther

> So far the exposition of the epistle of St. Paul to the Galatians. May the Lord Jesus Christ, our Justifier and Savior, who has granted me the grace and ability to expound this epistle and has granted you the grace and ability to hear it, preserve and confirm both you and me. From the heart I pray that we may grow more and more in the knowledge of grace and of faith in him, so that we may be blameless and beyond reproach until the day of our redemption. To him, with the Father and the Holy Spirit, be praise and glory forever and ever. Amen. (*Luther's Works*, Vol. 27, p. 144)

Soli Deo Gloria